I0643475

John Clifford

The English Baptists

Who they are and what they have done

John Clifford

The English Baptists
Who they are and what they have done

ISBN/EAN: 9783337202804

Printed in Europe, USA, Canada, Australia, Japan

Cover: Foto ©ninafisch / pixelio.de

More available books at **www.hansebooks.com**

THE ENGLISH BAPTISTS,

WHO THEY ARE, AND

WHAT THEY HAVE DONE.

Being Eight Lectures, Historical and Descriptive, given by General
Baptist Ministers in London, during the past winter.

EDITED BY

JOHN CLIFFORD, M.A., LL.B.

London:

E. MARLBOROUGH & CO., 51, OLD BAILEY.

1881.

Published under the Sanction of the General Baptist Publication Board.

CONTENTS.

PREFACE.

THESE lectures originated at a meeting of the G. B. M. F. :— which hieroglyphics being interpreted describe the London General Baptist Ministers' Fraternal : a gathering held once a month for good fellowship, friendly counsel, and sympathetic co-operation in Christian work.

The suggestion of such an effort as this is due to the fertile mind of our friend Mr. M'Cree. Some reasons urged, and accepted for it were, the interchange of services on week evenings by the ministers ; the development of a fraternal feeling in the churches ; the distribution of information amongst our younger members on topics not too often coming within the range of their reading ; and the production of a healthy and manly denominational enthusiasm. Those reasons vindicated the delivery of these Lectures ; and the two latter are sufficient warrant for their publication.

We have spoken of Baptists not because we think them perfect. We know them too well to cherish any such mistakes. Nor have we chosen this topic because we are vain ; at least we think not. We take no credit to ourselves for being Baptists. Some of us certainly would not have been such if we could have helped it. Talking after the manner of men, we could have done "better for ourselves" if we had helped it. But necessity was laid upon us. We are simply true. We have followed such light as we had and have striven to receive every ray that fell within our reach. And though we rejoice that we are Baptists and General Baptists, yet we rejoice far more in our fellowship with the holy Church throughout the world. We are Christians. We take our best and foremost name from Christ, a name, we are glad to add, that unites us with the good of all ages, and of all churches, and of all lands, with all who have sought, and with all who still seek, the best in character and the purest in service : and we hope to promote by this labour, the real welfare of that vast and far reaching spiritual community, the Universal Church.

It will not be forgotten that these are "popular lectures," not elaborate treatises. Much is omitted of necessity, and many points are discussed in a fragmentary way. Prof. Freeman says, in his "Growth of the English Constitution," "In a popular lecture, it is impossible to deal with everything with which it is desirable to deal; it is impossible to go to the bottom of those things which one picks out to deal with. It is enough—because it is all that can be done—if the choice of subjects is fairly well made, and if the treatment of those that are chosen, though necessarily inadequate, is accurate so far as it goes. Many things must be left out altogether; many things must be treated imperfectly; the attention of the hearer must be caught by putting some things in a more highly wrought shape than one would choose at another time. The object is gained if the lecturer awakens in his hearers a real interest in the subject on which he speaks, and if he sends them to the proper sources of more minute knowledge." We cannot hope to have fully realized this ideal of a popular lecture, but we have honestly striven to give accurate information, to present leading and typical facts, and to stimulate that loyalty to truth which shines with such radiance in the story of the English Baptists, and is, according to John Morley, "the mainstay of human advancement."

JOHN CLIFFORD.

THE

ORIGIN AND GROWTH OF ENGLISH BAPTISTS:

BY

JOHN CLIFFORD, M.A.

A T a Meeting of the Students of Yale College, Governor Bates, of Missouri, was called upon to make a speech. Several graduates had preceded him, each out-doing the other in eulogy of his illustrious *Alma Mater*. Mr. Bates, who had not received the benefits of University training, in rising, said, " Gentlemen, you all have the advantage of me. I have no *Alma Mater;* but this I can say,—that I came from a part of the country where they don't ask a man who his mother is ; but *what can you do?*" That latter question is the one addressed with persistent and increasing energy, to all Christian Churches in our day. It avails nothing to tell a practical and utilitarian age like this of a hoary ecclesiastical ancestry and a spotless apostolic descent. We must prove our right to exist by the perennial faithfulness of our lives, and make our "origin" an interesting theme by rendering our existence a benediction and a joy. What does it matter where a Church came from if it has lost its original inspiration—has no soothing words for bruised hearts, no eager sympathies and helpful fellowships, and no lever lifting the souls of men nearer to God, and truth, and righteousness! It is a doomed Church, let its "origin" be never so saintly, and its past growth never so extensive. It will die, as it ought, and the hurrying world will not interpose the slightest obstacle to its certain approach to its deserved fate.

Baptists, so far as I know them, welcome the most strenuous

application of this utilitarian test. They care less than most about denominational pedigrees and brilliant traditions. Their hearts beat with the throbbing life of the age. They are, for the most part, eager to do the work of to-day while the day lasts, and before it is too late, and are slow to take credit to themselves because they were born after their fathers. Their history is valued chiefly because it illumines the eternal principles of human progress, and breathes the refreshing inspirations of unchanging truth.

For the "past" is not really "dead," if the men are but alive who handle it. No doubt it is the present radiance of the sun that hangs a jewel on every grass-blade, and sows the earth at large with orient pearls, yet the consolidated heat-beams of far-back Carboniferous times, stored in the coal-seams of the globe, come forth at the touch of living men, and form one of the mightiest and most necessary forces of our active age. So it is the *living* Church, of any and of every name, that is doing Christ's redeeming and regenerating work amongst men ; but since He is not only the light of the present, but has also been the light of the past, therefore that past is the storehouse of some of the most beneficent energies living Christian men can use. For "History" is, according to a supreme witness, "the most profitable of all studies ;" forms "the message all mankind delivers to every man"; and Church History "is a sort of continued Holy Writ—our sacred books being, indeed, only a history of the primeval Church, as it first arose in man's soul and symbolically embodied itself in his external life."[*] We believe we do not make too large a claim when we assert that the story of "The Origin and Growth of the English Baptists," is a page of that "continued Holy Writ" which owes its fruitful existence to the ever-living Spirit Who guides and rules the universal Church for the perfection of individual character and the salvation of the world ; nor are we without a hope that the study of this subject, in some of its manifold aspects in this course of lectures, will be fraught with as much profit for others as it will have interest to ourselves.

---

[*] Carlyle's Miscellanies, vol. ii. p. 261.

I.—THE DIVINE ORIGINAL.

Everybody knows that, like most other Christians, Baptists claim to fashion their ideas and practices after the New Testament type ; but it is far more pertinent to note, that there are very few competent persons who dispute the legitimacy of their claim. Whatever else may be in the Church of the Apostolic age, or may be *developed* out of it, it is universally allowed, that the central, magnetic Baptist ideas are there, with unmistakable distinctness and reiterated emphasis. Jesus Himself was baptized ; and His disciples, in His name and as His representatives, baptized others. The Church of Pentecost was a community of Baptists. The eunuch heard Philip the deacon "preach Jesus," and forthwith asked for baptism as a personal privilege embraced within what he had just listened to, and from the enjoyment of which he was not to be debarred. Gentiles who had been baptized on becoming proselytes to the Jewish faith, were baptized again in the name of Jesus. Pagans called out of darkness into the marvellous light of the Gospel, signalized the divine event by their baptism.

New Testament baptisms, however, were in rivers, like the Jordan or Ænon, not in founts or basins, or by means of a few drops of water from a leathern bottle. There is no infant baptism in the Sacred Scriptures. Dr. Jacob, a scholar of unimpeachable eminence, and a clergyman in the established Church, wrote : " Notwithstanding all that has been written by learned men upon this subject, it remains undisputable that Infant Baptism is not mentioned in the New Testament. No instance of it is recorded there ; no allusion is made to its effects ; no directions are given for its administration. It ought to be distinctly acknowledged that it is not an apostolic ordinance."*

In short, there is not a Biblical exegete of high repute who does not admit that we are *exegetically right* in teaching that New Testament Baptism was a personal profession of personal trust in the personal Christ, of loyalty to His august authority, and of consecration to His blessed service. There is not a widely recognized ecclesiastical historian who denies that we are *histori-*

---

* Jacob's Ecclesiastical Polity of the New Testament, p. 270.

cally right in maintaining that the original copy of baptism contains in it the two elements of faith and immersion, and that the faith precedes the immersion ; and finally, there is not a student of the New Testament ordinances who does not allow we are *symbolically right* when we affirm, that New Testament baptism denotes that the believer in Christ had passed the crisis in which he broke with sin, and became "dead" to self-seeking and self-pleasing, and "alive unto God" and all His claims and gifts.

So that whatever may have happened since the death of the Apostle John— whatever changes and *developments* may have taken place, it is hardly to be denied that these phases of the Apostolic Church are clearly reproduced in the teaching and practice of those who inculcate—

1.—That " Salvation " is annexed to personal trust in Christ.
2.—That such trust takes precedence of, and qualifies for baptism.
3.—That such baptism is by immersion, and
4.—Signifies not less and not more than that the baptized person is already a believer in the Lord Jesus, consciously a recipient of the blessings of His sacrifice and resurrection, and is lovingly consecrated to the service of His Kingdom.

Thus we go at once to Jesus Christ, and to the Churches formed directly under the inspiration of His leadership at Jerusalem, Cesaræa, the Syrian Antioch, and Rome, for "the patterns of the things" after which we shape our life and construct our spiritual communities. Father Stand-fast said, when he was dying, "I have loved to hear my Lord spoken of ; and wherever I have seen the print of His shoe in the earth, there I have coveted to set my foot too." We believe and are sure that we see "the print of His shoe" in the institution of this ordinance, and in its beautiful teaching, and our love of Him Who *first* loved us and makes our hearts now glow with ardent regard for Him and His will, urges us to "covet to set our feet there too."

II.—Departures from the First Pattern.

But whatever is thought about our conformity to the Divine Original shown us in the Scriptures of the New Testament, *we* make no pretension to trace a distinct and unbroken ecclesiastical Baptist existence through all the centuries up to the Primitive Church of Paul and John. Indeed, supposing we had irrefragable evidence of the continuity of Baptists, it would do us no good ; it would not add a jot to our truthfulness, or a tittle to our usefulness. Moreover, we know, that Baptists, as an organized and reproductive body, having reportable lineal descendants and a corporate history, are of recent growth.

It is to be feared that *Baptist*, like other leading ideas of the New Testament Church, began to shine with a confused and flickering light soon after the close of the Apostolic age. Some critics assert that Irenæus (who was born about 126 A.D., accepted the pastorate of the Church at Lyons in 177, and died in 202), makes a passing allusion to the Baptism of infants, sufficient to prove that the practice was in existence in the middle of the second century, and recognised by one who was familiar with the Apostle John ; but over this reference we need not linger here, since such a competent *Pædobaptist* authority as Hagenbach, declares, in his *History of Doctrines*, that the statement in question "is no decisive proof" that "Infant Baptism had come into use in the primitive Church," but only "expresses the beautiful idea that Jesus was Redeemer *in* every stage of life, and *for* every stage of life."[*]

But, say what we will of the second century, it is evident that deep and wide-spread changes took place in the *third* century Church affecting its constitution, its polity, its theology, its ordinances, its spirituality, and its power. Infant Baptism became generally prevalent. Threefold immersion, which had become the universal method, gave place, under Eunomius (A.D. 360) to single immersion [†] ; and in the fifth century, sprinkling, which, according to Dean Stanley, had only been resorted to in cases of dangerous illness, became the customary practice in large sections of the Christian Church.[‡]

Nevertheless it is a matter of historical certainty, allowed by

---

[*] See Note A.
[†] Smith's Dictionary of Christian Antiquities, vol. I., 161.
[‡] Note B.

authorities whose judgment and accuracy are above suspicion, that
the essential Baptist ideas were fought for through these centuries
of thickening ecclesiastical mist, as true and divine, both by illustrious *individuals* such as Tertullian, Novatian, Paulinus, and the
Venerable Bede, and by *bodies* of Christians, such as the Euchites,
Novatians, Donatists, Waldenses, Lollards, and others.* And
authors, *not* Baptists, have gone so far as to maintain, that at
no time since the day of Pentecost have Baptist principles lacked
earnest adherents, and eager, though often persecuted, exponents.†

III.—BAPTISTS IN ENGLAND.

Be this so, or be it not, there is reason to believe, that when
Christianity came to our own country, it brought with it the
blinding haze and weakening confusion of the third and fourth
century Church, rather than the strong simplicity and " dry " light
of Apostolic days.   Of British Christianity in the time of the
ascendency of Imperial Rome, we have little more than plausible
guesses ; nor is there much of a different character concerning the
Saxon period.   Camden reports, in Fuller's *Church History,* that when
Augustine, who was sent to England by Pope Gregory in 596, "baptized
about 10,000 persons in the North, he commanded, by the voice of
criers, that the people should enter the river confidently, two by
two, and in the name of the Trinity, baptize one another by
turns."   Suggestive of similar ideas is the statement that
Paulinus, of York, the companion of Augustine, and sent by the
same Gregory in 601, baptized in the *rivers* Swale and Trent.
Bede, born in 672, historian of the Saxon Church, says, " Men
are first to be instructed in the knowledge of the truth,
then to be baptized as Christ hath taught, because without faith
it is impossible to please God ;" and he further affirms that the King
and Queen of the Northumbrians, having been instructed in the
word of Christ's salvation, " were washed in the river Glen as a
bath of remission."   The Waldenses, some of whom held Baptist
ideas, abounded in England in the days of William the Conqueror,
and Bishop Lanfranc wrote against the "heretics" in 1087.

---

* See Note C.   † See Note D.

It is likely that a *Church* formed on Baptist "lines" existed at Hillcliffe, a mile and a half from Warrington, as early as 1357, and it is certain that John Wycliffe, who was born in 1324, and died in 1384, was not far from the Baptist faith ; whilst it is notorious that many of the Lollards held and practised it with great daring and burning zeal. Herzog's Encyclopedia says, Henry VIII. executed fourteen Hollanders, accused as Anabaptists, in 1535, whilst ten others escaped by recanting ; and in the following year, certain Baptist *societies* in England, probably of Dutch origin, sent a deputation to a large gathering of the Anabaptists near Buckholt, in Westphalia.* Foxe says, a Baptist yeoman of the guard, at Windsor, suffered martyrdom under Queen Mary, and Bishop Jewel complains of the Antipædo-baptists in the time of Elizabeth "as a great and inauspicious crop ;"† and accordingly her Imperial Highness Queen Elizabeth commanded all Anabaptists to depart out of the kingdom within twenty-one days, England not being sufficiently large and free for such pestilent persons.‡

There is, therefore, no doubt (1) that the Christianity of Britain contained Baptist ideas within it from the beginning, as witness the practice of men like Augustine, and the teaching of Apostles, like the Venerable Bede : (2) that right onward to the closing years of Elizabeth's reign these "ideas" struggled with varying degrees of intensity to gain an organic shape and vital prominence in the religious life of the nation, and (3), owing mainly to a large accession of force from Dutch Baptists, actually found living expression in a few Baptist Societies in the fourteenth, fifteenth, and sixteenth centuries, as at Hillcliffe, in Cheshire ; Bocking, in Essex ; Faversham and Eycthorne, in Kent ; and Epworth and Crowle, in the Isle of Axholme.§ But the times were not favourable to the organizing of these sporadically distributed churches into a compact, coherent, and aggressive unity ; nor yet to the creation of any means by which they might

---

* Barclay. Life of the Relig. Soc. of the Commonwealth, p. 13-14.
† Stoughton's Ecc. Hist. (first edition), II. 234.
‡ McClintock and Story's Cyclo. of Bib. and Eccl. Lit. I. 653.
§ See Note E.

report their existence and doings to subsequent generations. Even in the days of Elizabeth, to be a Baptist was to be a criminal. The hour had not yet dawned for the emancipation of the human conscience. But it was coming : and the persecuted Baptist was privileged to take a momentous part in ushering in that sublime hour in the history and progress of the human race.

IV.--The Place of English Baptists in the Protestant Reformation.

The story of the "origin" of the English Baptists, is a vital portion of the records of one of the most thrilling and heroic eras in the history of the English people. It carries us into the midst of the fierce controversies, fine culture, grandly real beliefs, soul-impelling convictions, and great movements of the times of the strong-willed Elizabeth, the vain if not vacuous James, the vacillating Charles, and the brave and lion-hearted Cromwell, "the soul of the Puritan revolt." These were confessedly "stirring times" in the history of the upbuilding of the British people ; and though such Baptists as then existed were persecuted with a ghastly and tragic zeal, yet they were faithful, unselfish, and death-daring men ; plenteously endowed with the faults of temper characteristic of the age, but resolute and uncompromising in their search for truth, and doing a work that was real, inspired by exalted motives, and not wanting in a certain glow of divineness ; and therefore it is a work which counts for something in the sum of those forces that have helped to make the England and the world of this year, 1881 ; and "the soul of it remains part of the eternal soul of things."

You cannot rend the continuity of the centuries. To-day is the child of yesterday. To-morrow will be the growth of to-day and all preceding days. History is a unity, and every honest fight for principles has an eternal value. No men, whether few or many, solitary or crowd-surrounded, persecuted or petted, hidden in dark, dank prisons, banished into strange and inhospitable lands, or dwelling in the courts and palaces of the great, can engage in a manly effort to realise a Divine Idea, to obtain a larger and nobler spiritual life, to find out and hold God's everlasting Truth, without contributing real aid to humanity in its advances towards its divinely predestined goal. History is not made with *éclat.* It does not sound a trumpet before it, like the Pharisees. Men live and think, sigh, suffer and pray, speak and toil, do, dare, and die, and the great life of humanity moves forward, huge problems are solved, and abiding and universally valuable results are secured. Of all the men living on our isle at the close of the sixteenth and at the dawning of the seventeenth centuries, the Baptists, or Anabaptists, as they were then called, were the most despised and the most hated, and yet they were making one of the most solid and valuable contributions to the commercial, political, and spiritual progress of Great Britain and the world.

(1.) For the story of the "origin" of the English Baptists is a chapter in the struggle of English Christians to discover for themselves, from the Scriptures, and to put into shape, THE DIVINE IDEA OF A VISIBLE CHRISTIAN CHURCH. The people who are called Baptists came into existence as the logical and inevitable result of an attempt, on the part of believers in Christ in this realm, to purify and develop England's life, to set its parishes free from practical ungodliness, by supplying, amongst other things, a true answer to the questions, *What is a Christian Church? and of what kind of persons ought it to consist?* The chief motive was the purification of the Church of God ; and the capital method was a true and practical definition of the New Testament Church.

At that time there was no question of equal gravity. It was the "blazing" subject of the hour. No topic required so much daring in those who handled it ; so much steadfast heroism in those who were prepared to follow their answer to its legitimate issues. It was a new question, and it was as revolutionary as it was new. Merely to put it suggested to many minds the profanest hardihood, and lifted whirlwinds of scorn. Ineffably worse was it then to ask, " Is the State Church the New Testament Church ?" "Ought all parishioners to be Church members ?" than it is to ask to-day, "Is there a God ?" "Is the Bible true ?" "Is Christianity historically verifiable ?" And the men who put the enquiry had to be ready for banishment to the wilds of America, or the more genial refuge of Holland, or even for martyrdom, if the response they found carried them into opposition to the reigning notions of the hour, and to the state-supported and state-defended religious institutions of the day.

Do not let us disguise this fact. Whatever English Baptists may be and do *now*, it is certain their ORIGIN is *not* due to the quiet investigation of two or three passages of Scripture concerning the way in which believers in Christ should be baptized ; whether by sprinkling, by pouring, or by dipping ; whether once or three times ; nor to the rejection of infant baptism ; nor even to the denial of the magical sacramental efficacy of baptism ; it goes far deeper, and includes immeasurably more. The Baptist Church sprang into being, as other churches did in that day—not from wild fanaticism ; not from excessive vanity ; not from questions of much or little water in a rite, but from unswerving loyalty to God ; from a profoundly religious effort to form a *visible Christian Church after the idea and according to the teaching of the Lord Jesus Christ Himself.* It was a real human struggle for the realization of divine ideas, born out of the love of God and the desire for the establishment of His reign upon earth. Baptist history is therefore a bush aflame with the presence of God, and the ground it covers is not less holy than that on which Moses, with bared feet, stood hopeful, yet trembling, as near to the God of Israel.

(2.) The story of the "origin" of the English Baptists, is, then, a *fragment* of the larger story of the "English Reformation," and takes rank by the side of those sections of our country's history which narrate the rise of Protestantism ; the appearance and work of the Puritans; the origin and progress of the Separatists and Brownists, Independents and "Quakers." The religious spirit was supreme—it dominated everywhere. William Tyndall* had fanned into a flame the smouldering embers of Lollardism, and roused into newness of life and baptized with fresh energy, the work of the illustrious John Wycliffe, by sending forth the New Testament in a version which, in substance, is still in use amongst us. Luther's famous defence of faith and purity at Wittenberg

---

* 'Born at Nibley, Gloucestershire, 1477 ; sent out his New Testament in 1525, and was burned to death, after a protracted imprisonment, in September, 1536.

had resounded throughout Europe like a peal of thunder echoing amongst the Alpine hills ; and had stirred an enthusiasm hardly second to that of the Crusades.* Protestantism was rapidly taking shape in England ; but under such dubious circumstances, and with so many questionable surroundings, royal, ecclesiastic, and theological, that it had not long existed, before there grew by the side of it, if not actually from it, a *second* Protestantism, with a sharper accent, a more decided ring, carrying the revolt against the paganized Christianity of the Papacy to a further extreme. The *first* protest was mainly against the *Pope* of Rome and his jurisdiction in these realms. The *second* protest was an endorsement of the first, but it went beyond it, and protested with even a stronger vehemence against copes, stoles, and altars, and the priestly dogmas, practices, and paraphernalia of the Roman Catholic hierarchy. Protestantism had positively and inevitably protested itself into Puritanism.

(3.) It could not help it. It must be so. Protestantism was essentially and centrally the beginning of a return to the *Divine Original* of Christian faith and practice in the Scriptures; and once on that road, Protestantism could not be a finality. PURITANISM was the logical issue of the Protestant spirit. "One of the noblest heroisms ever transacted on this earth," owed its rise to the appeal to the Scriptures; and its surprising energy and rapid progress were also due to the tremendous impulse given to the religious life of the nation, about the middle of Elizabeth's reign, by the circulation of those same Holy Scriptures. The Bible became the chief literature of England ; its fable and its history, its poetry and its philosophy, its manual of practice and its guide and inspiration to devotion— so that Grotius said of this country, ten years after the Queen's death, " Theology rules there ;" and Professor Green affirms that, " the whole nation had become, in fact, a Church."†

But the Puritan protest was restricted to men who still belonged to the English Parliamentary Church, and whose one aim was not to

---

* Luther was born in 1483; published his Theses against Indulgences, at Wittenberg, in 1517 ; burned the Pope's Bull in 1520 ; died in 1546.

† History of the English People, 449.

leave that Church and substitute a better, but to stay in and gradually purify it, and, indeed, Calvinize, *i.e.*, Presbyterianize it. Just as in the English Church of this day, there are many who bitterly denounce the Romanist practices of the Ritualistic Clergy, and yet are content to minister in an institution which has done more, the last forty years, to foster and develop Roman Catholicism in England, than all other forces and institutions put together, so the majority of the Puritans were at first ready to regard the Church of Henry and Elizabeth, as a true visible Church of Jesus Christ, and directed their opposition mainly against certain practices and theories, being themselves ever intent on maintaining its integrity, and perfecting its methods.

(4.) But the Biblical and Spiritual forces at work in the English nation, revolutionizing its religious ideas and practices, could not stop there. As the first protest led on to the second, so the second led on a *third.*

Puritanism advanced to SEPARATISM. Bodies of men appeared who were unwilling to admit that the Church of England, even if reformed according to the Genevan pattern, was a true Church of Christ. A deeper Reformation was requisite than a change of dress and of ritual. *The terms of membership required alteration.* "It is contrary," said the Separatists, "to the will of Christ that the area of the Church should be fixed by the area of the land. We are profoundly convinced that the practical reform of the spiritual life of England can never be realized in connection with that parochial system of churches which considers all baptized persons to be redeemed children of God, until excommunication has furnished proof to the contrary." Thus a *third* form of Protestantism arose, more advanced than the second, and inculcating the necessity of forming "particular churches." Led by Robert Browne, an "erratic individual," (according to Fuller and Masson); Henry Barrowe, Francis Johnson, John Penry, John Greenwood, and Henry Jacob, such separated churches grew exceedingly, and according to Green, numbered 20,000 souls in the middle of Elizabeth's reign.* Some of these churches were

---

* Green, Hist. Eng. People, 459.

called Brownists, after Robert Browne, and subsequently Independents, from their assertion of the sufficiency of the Church to care for and govern itself, and their death-defying insistance upon the principle that the Church of Christ ought not, and could not, consist of any but those who were really believers in Him, and avowedly subject to His authority. They vehemently opposed the pernicious doctrine of sponsorship,* and would not accept the theory of Whitgift and Hooker, that the nation makes the Church, and that being born in a parish of the nation gives a right to be in the Church of Christ. Strongly, and even fiercely, they denounced the deed by which "in one day, with the blast of Queen Elizabeth's trumpet," ignorant papists and gross idolaters were made faithful Christians and true professors.† The unit of the Church of Christ is, and always must be, a Christian man.

(5). Now out of these Separatists, with their cardinal principle that the members of a New Testament Church should be Christians, grew logically and inevitably the ENGLISH BAPTISTS. The first protest was against Romanism as concentrated in a Pope, and subjecting the King of this land to his authority ; the second protest was against all papal practices, and in favour of getting rid of a prelacy and bringing in synodical authority ; the third protest was against the inclusion of all the subjects of the King in the Church, irrespective of their spiritual character and in favour, ultimately, of the self-governing powers of each separate Christian Society ; but still, INFANTS were included, at least the infants of Christian parents, and yet how could they be personally conscious Christians ? how could they aid in the government of a church ? what spiritual character had they to qualify them for membership ? It was certain as to-morrow that a FOURTH PROTEST should come. The forces of the living Word, and of their own faith impelled them to oppose the inclusion of any persons in the Church of Christ Jesus, excepting such as intelligently, and consciously received Him, and were possessed of His divine life. THAT FOURTH PROTEST WAS MADE BY THE ENGLISH

---

* Dexter, H. L., Dr., Congregationalism as seen in its Literature, 77.
† Henry Barrowe's Brief Description of the False Church (1590) p. 10.

BAPTISTS AND IS THEIR HISTORICAL ROOT. To cite the language of one of these, they reasoned thus, "The Separation must either go back to England, (*i.e.*, the English Church), or forward to true Baptism ; all that shall in time to come separate from England must separate from the baptism of England ; and if they will not separate from the Baptism of England, there is no reason why they should separate from England as from a false Church." Right as far as they went, yet the Separatists and Independents did not go far enough to satisfy these root and branch men. They had got firm grip of a principle, and they were willing to go with it wherever it might take them. They were contending for eternal realities. The battle was not about words, but spiritual facts. Christ Jesus was central to His Church, and a living personal and conscious relation to Him was the fundamental condition of fellowship in His societies. Personal faith in, and personal subjection to, the Lord Jesus, is all and in all. But faith is a conscious act. It requires intelligence. It involves will. It is not possible to a babe ; therefore babes have no more right in the Church of the New Testament because they are born in a Christian family, than Englishmen have perforce a right in the Church because they are born in a Christian parish. The principle which excludes the parishioner allows no place to the -babe. So they reasoned, so they felt and acted, and thus English Baptists came into being as a vital and enduring product of the Great Protestant Reformation, and in fact advancing that Reform a stage further than it had before marched, but along its own original lines of the pre-eminence of the Scriptures, and the absolute necessity of a really personal godliness. It was a logical and conclusive application of the governing rules and controlling spirit of Puritanism, carrying, if we may mathematically express it, Protestantism up to its fifth power, as a denial of the right of men to substitute any merely external conditions and accidental circumstances, for a living, sincere, and real faith in Christ, and a hearty personal subjection to His august authority.*

---

* The genealogical tree of the English Baptists may therefore be expressed thus, beginning with the root.—I. PROTESTANTS, II. PURITANS,

VI.—John Smyth and the English Baptists.

The man who illustrates these successive stages in the history
of the Protestant Reformation in his own career, and holds one of
the most memorable names in the Baptist annals, is John Smyth,
Vicar of Gainsborough. Standing at the head of distinctly consecu-
tive Baptist history, he may be regarded as the father and founder
of the organized Baptists of England ; and of the General
Baptists specially and primarily. Like not a few of the Separatists he was a Cambridge man, matriculated as a prizeman of
Christ's College in 1571, took his B.A. in 1575-6, was elected
a Fellow, and commenced his M.A. in 1579 ; afterwards he was
lecturer at Lincoln, and then became Vicar of Gainsborough, on
the Trent. Seized by the Time-Spirit he was restless and
agitated, earnest and thoroughgoing. At the University he was
cited before the Vice-Chancellor for vindicating the Sabbath day
from the profanation of "Sports," and he was not likely to be
long before coming into collision with the high-handed ecclesiastical authorities for his zeal as a Reformer. Protestantism was
not enough for him, and slow as he was in making up his mind,
yet his relentless pursuit of truth forbade him finding content in
mere Puritanism. For "nine months "he was perplexed "about the
separation," and betook himself to the house of Sir William Bowes
at Coventry, to confer with such noted Puritan leaders as Dod,
Hildersham, and Barbour, but this long "disputation" did not
bring him satisfaction. Though not without misgiving, he still
clung to the National Church, meanwhile fearlessly seeking the
truth, and forming his convictions. His supreme duty was not
to be consistent ; it was to be true, and so, faithful to his convictions, he went forward, and at length became pastor of a church
formed on the Separatist, or Independent type, in the year 1602.

But that stage was not final. At Crowle, in Lincolnshire, a
few miles from Gainsborough, there was, according to an old Church

---

III. Separatists, IV. Independents, V. Baptists. The "Friends,"
or Quakers have passed on beyond the Baptists, and abolished all ordinances whatever. They are not only subsequent to the Baptists, but drew
their numbers very largely from amongst the General Baptists. — See
W. Tallack on "George Fox, and the Early Baptists."

book, recently copied, a Baptist Society as early as 1599.* To
that rural community Smyth went in the year 1604, and "debated
nearly all night with Elders Henry Helwise and John Morton, who
defended our cause well." Not yet, however, was he convinced,
but after three months reflection, his mind had advanced beyond
the position of the Separatists. He had, says the Church book,
"consulted the Scriptures, and admitted that he was deceived in
the way of Pædo-baptistry," and "so embraced the faith in a true
Christian and Apostolic baptism," and on the "24th of March, 1606,
at midnight," to avoid the satellites of the persecuting Church, and
under the glare of torchlight, "he was baptised by Elder John
Morton, in the river Don, and then walked to Epworth, a distance
of two miles, in his wet clothes."

These were terribly perilous times for men who dared to think,
speak, and act differently from the legalized religion. Puritanism
was beaten and chagrined at the Hampton Court Conference
of 1604, and King James, in his absolutism, had declared that he,
would "harry the Puritans out of the country, if they would not
conform." The separatists "were hunted and persecuted on every
side." None befriended them. "Some were taken and clapped
in prison ; others had their houses beset and watched night and
day [by apparitors and pursuivants], and hardly escaped their
hands ; and the most were fain to flee, and leave their houses and
habitations and means of their livelihood." Separatists, Brownists,
and Barrowists had heard and accepted the glad tidings that a
few leagues distant from the fens of Lincolnshire, there was a
country where "the Church was without a bishop and the state
without a king," and "freedom of religion was given to all men."
"John Smyth and his company" followed their example, and left
England for that paradise of religion, the Low Countries, and in
Amsterdam he supported himself by practising physic, "taking,"
as he says, "nothing of the poorer sort, and if they were rich, he
took half as much as other doctors did, except some who were
well able and well minded, urged more upon him," which we fear
they did not, for he seems to have lived on very humble fare ;

---

* See Note F.

and reminds us of his fellow-sufferer Ainsworth, who, being "a fine scholar," and the most profoundly learned of all the Brownists, lived in that same city, "upon nine-pence a week and some boiled roots."

But Smyth had other work than that of a doctor. Although he had found freedom, he had descended upon strange quarters, and strange folk. The Separatist Church was in a sadly perplexed and violently agitated state. All the faults of the Puritan temper had free course. Opinions gravitated towards extravagance, and crotchets were exalted into first principles. Disputes ran high. "The whalebone of Mrs. Johnson's (the Pastor's wife) too fashionable bodice, and the corks of her high-heeled shoes," had been matter of grave Church discipline. The awful power of excommunication had been wielded. Defamatory pamphlets had been flying in the air like shots at a rifle practice. The atmosphere was super-charged with the electricity of theological and ecclesiastical discussion. Moreover,—and this is a critical item for John Smyth —since 1591, James Arminius had been teaching his theology in opposition to Gomarus; and the Church of the Separatists, under pastor Ainsworth, had contended against that "damnable" faith. [*]

Was it likely John Smyth, with his courageous quest for truth, his unreserved fidelity to conviction, and his magnetic personal enthusiasm, would dwell long in the midst of such conditions without marking out a course for himself, and carrying others away with him in his fervid zeal. No ; he accepted an Arminian theology ; proclaimed an Antipædo-baptist view of baptism, held " no part of saving righteousness to consist in outward ceremonies," and disputed, at large—very much at large, it is to be believed— on questions of Church polity and Christian worship ; the issue of which was, that he, with a considerable body of followers, seceded and formed themselves into a Church, published "a confession of Faith," in twenty-six articles, approximating closer than any other to the General Baptist pattern. Smyth died in 1612 ; and Thomas Helwys, who had been associated with him in the direction of the Amsterdam society, came over to London, together

---

* See Note G.

with a company of his believing comrades; and to their hearty union, courageous labours, advanced principles, and accumulated sufferings, in 1611 and onwards, must be traced the origin of the General Baptist Connexion.

Obscure, confused, and contradictory as the notices of Smyth's history are, it is clear that he was a man of noble make, of fine spirit, and incorruptible sincerity. He had what lazy people call a "restless mind ;" and, in the opinion of selfish persons, he was "reckless" as to his own interests. Eager to follow the light as he saw it, he was daring enough to avow his successive changes of opinion. What mattered it to him that he thought differently yesterday ? His business was not to repeat yesterday, but to be true to-day. The Anglican Church was wrong, and therefore he left it, though it was dear to him as a mother. The Brownists had more light than the English Church, but he saw truth farther afield, and he went towards it, and became a Baptist—and a Baptist cherishing a theology broad and clear, tender and strong. Listen to his manly confession :—

"Although in this writing, something there is which over-thwarteth my former judgment in some treatises by me formerly published, yet I would intreat the reader not to impute that as a fault unto mee ; rather, it should be accounted a virtue to retract errors. Know, therefore, that latter thoughts oft-tymes are better than the former ; and I do professe this (that no man account it strannge): that I will every day, as my errors shall be discovered, confesse them and renounce them."*

That splendid conscientiousness was matched by a beautiful humility and a glowing charity. I know he had (as we all have), the faults of his virtues, and the errors of his time. He was incapable of theological perspective, disputative, and crotchety ; but he did not assume to himself a "plenary knowledge and assurance." He was ready to be taught, and was full of charity towards all who differed from him. A more potent witness to his beautiful personal qualities cannot be desired than the " Declaration " made by those from whom he seceded. Read in the light

---

* Differences of the Churches of the Separation, etc. iv.

of those days, it is one of the most eloquent panegyrics ever pronounced. "What," say they, "would we not have endured or done; would we not have lost all we had? would we not have plucked out our own eyes? would we not have laid down our lives (could we still in conscience have enjoyed and followed his teaching), doth not God know this? Do not men know it? Doth he not know it? Have we not neglected ourselves, our wives, our children, and all we had, and respected him? And we confess we had good cause so to do in respect of those most excellent gifts and graces of God that then did abound in him; and all our love was too little for him and not worthy of him."* Norman Macleod wished to be "broad as the charity of Almighty God,........." and "narrow as His righteousness." Faulty in many things as John Smyth undoubtedly was, yet we claim for him that he was an admirable exemplification of this spirit, and not an unworthy illustration of the best men in one of the best eras of our British life.

The same principles are embodied in the origin of the first distinctively PARTICULAR, or CALVINISTIC BAPTIST CHURCH. Its date is given with precision, and the circumstances of its formation are clearly reported. Even the day is mentioned. It was Sep. 12, 1633. No doubt a good number of churches of the *General* Baptist order holding Arminian views, came into existence during the prior twenty years; but the Church at Broad Street, Wapping, was not directly connected with, or derived from, any of them. It grew, as William Kiffin tells us, out of an Independent Church (in the way we have described) which was formed in London in 1616, and was under the pastorate of Henry Jacob. The subject of the baptism of infants pushed itself forward as they read the Scriptures, and they reasoned thereupon, and urged, partly by that, and partly by the consideration that they were too numerous to meet together secretly, as was necessary, a score of men and women, "with divers others;"† whatever that may mean, seceded and formed a new Church on Baptist "lines," but with a Particular, or Calvinistic, Theology, electing to the pastorate Mr. JOHN

---

* A Declaration of the Faith of English people remaining at Amsterdam.
† Crosby, I. 1.

SPILSBURY, a man of high repute amongst his brethren, and one of the Early Baptist Leaders.

That was the year in which William Prynne, as Carlyle reminds us, was "brought to the Star Chamber, to the pillory, and had his ears cropped off for the first time; who also, strange as it may look, manifested no gratitude, but on the contrary, for all that trouble."* It was the year in which the little Dr. Laud was executing with terrible emphasis his measures for the total suppression of Puritanism, and the year in which a denomination was born that has exhibited that same Puritanism, in its essential strength and conquering energy, not only in this, but also in many other lands.

VII.—BAPTIST GROWTH.

(1.) FROM 1611 TO 1688.

So long as Puritanism retained its original force, and persecution kept the fires of its malignity in full blaze, " the Word of the Lord " among Baptists grew and multiplied. Hence, from the days of John Smyth to the time of William of Orange, the course of the General Baptists was one of bitter suffering, noble testimony, and conspicuous prosperity. Fiercely assaulted and heavily oppressed, they clung to each other with a heartier love, saw the truth with clearer vision, and propagated their opinions with increasing zeal, and irrepressible devotion. Under the leadership of men of such heroic temper as Thomas Helwys, Leonard Busher, Thomas Lamb, Henry Denne, and Samuel Oates,† they developed a host of fearless confessors, and contributed not a few serviceable books. Their own liberties being restricted, they saw the need for a free gospel, a free worship, a free church, a free State, and a free conscience. And what they saw they proclaimed. The Seer became the Apostle. They were the first to state with distinctness and energy the great modern doctrine of "Liberty of Conscience;" and from a "dingy" General Baptist "meeting-house somewhere in Old London," in 1614,

---

* Oliver Cromwell, I, 45 and 63.

† *Cf.* Lecture by W. Harvey Smith on "Seventeenth Century Baptists."

"there flashed out first in England the absolute doctrine of Religious Liberty."*

This brave proclamation of freedom and of truth was magnetic. It cast a spell over men. "Multitudes of disciples" gathered about them. General Baptist Churches sprang up in the East and West and Midlands, as well as in London and the South. At Yarmouth, in Norfolk; Stony Stratford and Amersham, in Bucks; Ashford, in Kent; Tiverton, in Devon; and many other places, congregations were gathered and the word of the Lord diffused. Men had got back to primitive truth and convictions, and, in spite of overwhelming persecutions, they continued to advance.

For England was not now the whole planet. A new world had been created, and a new and nobler England was being born. ROGER WILLIAMS,† a clergyman of the Established Church, was in the track of John Smyth. He too had become a Puritan, and had abandoned "holy orders;" and he embarked for America in 1630, and there took rank (showing the influences of the dingy meeting-house doctrines) not only as the founder of the first Baptist Church, but also as the first *legislator* who provided for full and free and absolute liberty of conscience; thus planting the seed which, on the one hand, has grown up into the strong, aggressive, and conquering Republic of the West, and on the other, into the largest religious denomination contained within that Republic.

Three years after Roger Williams sailed for America, as we have seen, the first Particular Baptist Church was formed. The same year saw the first Welsh Baptist Church come into existence at Olchon, on the borders of Wales. Soon afterwards Baptists spread into Ireland and Scotland; and in London they were so formidable a body by 1644, that the Lord Mayor thought fit to stop a public dispute‡, and in the following year, no less than forty-seven Baptist churches § were reported as existing in London alone, the majority of these, no doubt, being General Baptists; for, in 1644,

---

* Professor Masson, but see Note II.
† Born in Wales, in 1604; reared in London and Oxford; founder of Rhode Island, United States.
‡ Stoughton's Ecc. Hist. II. 237.
§ Wall's Infant Baptism.

only seven Metropolitan Particular Baptist churches were found to join in a memorable confession of faith addressed to Parliament, and to the ignorant, in reply to the aspersions unjustly cast upon the Baptists.*

Cromwell was favourable to our predecessors. They were in his army when he fought the King near Market Harborough and pursued him towards Leicester, in 1645, and Oliver says they were "honest men, who did their work faithfully."† Later still, Cromwell's "Triers" passed clergymen holding the Baptist ideas "as brethren," and the names of thirty-five Baptist ministers occur as holding livings at the restoration of Charles the Second, ‡ Thomas Grantham being witness, General Baptists alone had increased in their first fifty years to 20,000. Cramp says, in 1660, Baptist "churches existed in thirty English counties, were numerous in Wales, and occupied the principal towns of Ireland."§

Persecution was renewed with intolerable fierceness under Charles the Second, and reigned with intermittent but tremendous violence from 1660 to 1688. Dissenters were not allowed to meet in public : and could only steal occasions for fellowship and teaching—under the shelter of forest trees, or in the quiet of private homes. The State was bent on their extinction. Families were ruined. Houses were desolated. Estates were impoverished. Many fled to freer climes. Eight thousand perished in the prisons : and yet the more they were persecuted, the more they grew. Thomas Granthan, whose work ceased in 1692, said that the General Baptists had increased 10,000 since the second year of the restored Charles, so that, though they were scattered in rural districts, and had changed ther centre from London to an obscure spot, like Fenstanton, yet they now numbered 30,000. The Particular Baptist churches had been considerably reinforced by an accession of learned Calvinistic clergymen from amongst the "ejected," which gave an impetus to their progress, and so had they extended, that in 1689, a Confession of Faith was published,

---

* Confessions of Faith, pp. 13–48. Hanserd Knollys Society.
† Carlyle's Cromwell I. 193.
‡ Stoughton's Ecc. Lit. II. 239–242.
§ History of the Baptists, p. 281.

representing, as they themselves said, upwards of *one hundred baptized* congregations in England and Wales (denying *Arminianism*)," and signed by such honoured names as Hanserd Knollys, William Kiffin, and Andrew Gifford. Thus, in a little more than half a century, the one Church in Wapping had become more than a hundred churches, dispersed through England and Wales. We may therefore conclude that the FIRST PERIOD of organized British Baptist life, was one of solid and extensive growth in numbers and influence, in the conception and development of great principles, in patient energy, and in evangelistic activity.

(2.) FROM 1688 TO 1770.

A.D. 1688 is one of the most significant dates in the history of Britain, and, indeed, of Europe and the world, whether viewed in relation to the rise and establishment of revolutionary political principles, or to the chequered fortunes of religion. "The Glorious Revolution," as we still call the momentous change which centres in the arrival of William of Orange at Torbay, on the fifth of November, 1688, shattered the power of Roman Catholicism on the Continent ; saved England from the cruel tyranny and fierce corruptions of the Papacy ; substituted the sovereignty of the House of Commons for that of a King or Queen ; inaugurated the era of those "Great Commoners," of whom Robert Walpole was the first, and Mr. Gladstone is, at present, the most consummately able and accomplished, and, far ahead, the most lofty in genius, spirit, and character ; and finally, brought to the much-enduring Dissenters, the long-coveted boon of "freedom to worship God according to the dictates of their own consciences." The sun of political prosperity rose high in mid-heaven ; the sky was swept clean of its most maleficent elements, and a far freer course was given to the religious energy of the nation, than it had hitherto enjoyed.

But strange is the irony of life ! The era of religious freedom ushers in a fearful and wide-spread suppression of spiritual life, and a general torpor and decay amongst the Churches. Universal toleration is the attractive preface to the "intolerable" eighteenth century, with its rose-water imbecilities, washed-out convictions, rank corruptions, and increasing vice. Puritanism, alas ! became defunct. Its grand ideal was discredited and disgraced. The "age of faith" and of sublime heroisms, divine patiences, and majestic meeknesses, and heavenly serenities, gave place to an age of acute reasoning, subtle speculations, and everlasting grinding of "logic mills." Christianity became itself a hard and acrid syllogism instead of a rich and inspiring life. It existed as a whetstone to sharpen men's wits, not as a mystic angel to strengthen and beautify men's souls. "The creation of the world," said Usher the archbishop, with an irritating precision, "was finished on the 3rd of September, on a Wednesday." Why did he not add, "at 5, 55', 59", p.m.!" Men could not rise higher than the Socinian conception of Christ. Unitarianism spread so rapidly amongst the Presbyterians, that the English branch of that body was nearly extinguished; and the Episcopal community was so much more disputatious than evangelistic, that only one Church was erected in London and its neighbourhood, during fifty-five years—(1675 to 1730.)*

The strong free spirit of Puritanism had two courses before it. It ought to have elected a career of philanthropic work—of sympathy with the poor and the ignorant, and help for the needy, and become the chief healer of the physical and spiritual maladies of society. Instead of that, it chose to talk and debate, and died of it, as was meet.

Added to this gigantic blunder of Puritanism, there were other influences sapping the moral strength, and enfeebling the spiritual sinew of the nation. Walpole was a gifted financier, an ardent friend of peace, a true helper of commerce, and a wise champion of the Revolution, but he despised virtue, and laughed at appeals to the loftier and purer motives of human action as "School-boy flights," scorned by men of experience. So he helped to deteriorate the morals of the nation, though he fostered its wealth; and corrupted its best and highest life, though he gave solid splendour to the English name, and just and wide influence to English opinion. Coincidently there was the rise of British manufactures into a front and governing position. The Colonies stood open with their

---

* Barclay, Religious Societies of the Commonwealth, 516.

young and eager life. Large towns were increasing. Manchester and Birmingham doubled their population in thirty years, and Liverpool leapt from a village to the rank of third port in the kingdom. In fact, the golden era sung by poets had arrived, and Peace and Prosperity met together, Intellect and Wealth kissed each other. Or seen from a loftier height, the outer and inner life of the nation presented two pictures ;—inside, there was endless disputation about words to no profit, and little practical godliness ; and outside, there was the glitter of increasing wealth added to the subtle temptation of corruption in high places. It was inevitable that the best life of the nation should decay.

Baptists did not escape the contagion, and General Baptists, for reasons easily understood, suffered acutely and long.* Dissent being tolerated they had not to fight for their liberties ; what should they do with their skilled forces but fight one another about the imposition of hands ; about Arianism, and Socinianism, and Trinitarianism ! And this they did with a will, and with the usual desolating effect. Nonconformists forgot the grounds of their Nonconformity ; Baptists ceased to care whether they were "Particular" or "General," and not a few " Generals " passed over to the " Particulars " on the one hand, and to the " Quakers " on the other. Neal speaks of only 247 Baptist congregations in England and Wales in 1715, and Josiah Thompson mentions but 390 in 1772 ; whilst in London, in 1738, the General Baptist churches were reduced to nine, and the Particular Baptists that had been so largely favoured during Restoration times by the services of such men as Kiffin, and Knollys, and Bunyan, only numbered twenty-six,† fully proving that the Second Period of organic English Baptist Life though one of exceptional outward advantage compared with the first, was unspeakably inferior to it in all the high qualities of a living and aggressive Christian Church.

---

* See Note I.

† Maitland's History of England, p. 517, quoted in *Freeman* of May 13, 1881.

(3.) FROM 1770 TO 1850.

The year 1770 marks an epoch of special interest to General Baptists; for in the month of June of that year, Dan Taylor,* the brave, heroic Saint Dan, of immortal memory, co-operated with a few other earnest souls in forming the NEW CONNEXION OF GENERAL BAPTISTS, in Church Lane Chapel, Commercial Road, "with the design," as they themselves said, "to revive experimental religion, or primitive Christianity, in faith and practice."

So thoroughly had the defective theology, excessive disputatiousness and spiritual torpor of the age, penetrated the General Baptist Churches, that this "new departure" was absolutely necessary. Eleven ministers of the Old Connexion, representing 728 members in eleven churches, met eight ministers belonging to five *new* churches, containing 900 members, discussed the grounds of secession, and agreed upon "the Articles of Religion" which they were prepared to practise. The churches of the ancient order were located in London, Kent, Essex, and Yorkshire; those of the new type came from Barton and Kegworth, Loughborough, Longford, and Melbourne, and had started as *Independents*, but, purely by the study of the Scriptures, had been led to accept and avow General Baptist ideas.†

But, it must be remembered, those General Baptists were, and their successors of 1881 are, the offspring of that great Evangelical Revival, which, while it has created Methodism as its most conspicuous monument and memorial, has also sent its refreshing streams through all the churches, and begotten the Modern England in which we live. Dan Taylor began as a Methodist in Yorkshire, and David Taylor was a servant of Lady Huntingdon's, at Donington, in Leicestershire, who, by his village preaching, originated the Barton Church. The theological affinities of Methodism with General Baptist teaching formed a convenient and capable conductor for the regenerating influence of that mighty Renovation; thereby preventing the extinction of the General Baptists, and giving them a new beginning under new and better conditions, and with new life.

---

* *Cf.* J. Fletcher on "Dan Taylor and the English Baptists."
† See Note J.

Independents and Baptists generally looked shyly on the Revival at first, and gained little from it. But gradually it reached them, and Foreign Missions were originated before the century closed, Antinomianism was suppressed, their theology modified,* and philanthropic work was undertaken. Still it seems Baptist advance was by no means rapid, for between the years 1738—1816, *i.e.* in nearly 80 years, the London churches had only grown from thirty-five to forty-one,† and, according to Dr. Cramp, the number of churches in Great Britian and Ireland at this period somewhat exceeded 400, containing probably about 20,000 members,‡ *i.e.* all Baptists did not count more than the General Baptists, at the beginning of Charles the Second's reign, and 10,000 less than they numbered at the end of his career.

But the Evangelical leaven was at work, and signal progress was made in the next forty years. Three colleges for the training of men for the Baptist Ministry were started within six years, (Rawdon, Pontypool, and Regent's Park). Work for the heathen began to re-act powerfully at home, and at the middle of this century the London Churches had doubled in number, the General Baptists had grown from 1,628 members in 1770, to 18,277, and the Baptists of Great Britain and Ireland are returned at 100,391. Clearly the sun of prosperity had risen with special radiance and luminous promise upon the English Baptists, at the close of this, the THIRD PERIOD of their organized existence.

FROM 1850 TO 1880.

I cannot linger to signalize the principal features in the growth of the last thirty years, and sketch the *present status* of Baptists all over the world. Such a theme demands another lecture; but I may say, there has been advance of all kinds, all along the line, during the last quarter of a century, and most notably since the advent of the prodigious influence of the Rev. CHARLES HADDON SPURGEON. His is the most pronounced Baptist force of the last quarter of a century. His works are as

---

* See Note K.
† Ivimey's Constitution of the Baptist Churches, appendix, 1816.
‡ Cramp. History, 741.

abundant as his position is unique.   The enthusiasm of the great Evangelical Revival reappears in him ; and the strong passion for "saving souls,"characteristic of Whitfield,is supreme. But he has at the same time the practical and organizing skill of Wesley, and is the centre of a splendid system of energetic and evangelistic benefi- cence.   Theologically, he claims to stand by Calvin ; but he will leave Calvin, and all the theologies, to bring a man to Christ, and to extend the kingdom of the Lord Jesus.   As no work has been marked with more faith or zeal, tact or daring than his, so none has been more reproductive.   "Spurgeon's men " are going all over the planet ; and the number of church members represented at the last Conference of the Spurgeonic section of Baptists,reached the total of 44,505, *i.e.,* nearly a sixth of the whole denomination.

The numerical increase of this FOURTH PERIOD is a cheering feature.   227 Churches exist in London, where a quarter of a cen- tury ago were only 130.   The returns of Baptists of all kinds, for Great Britain and Ireland, are given as 281,061.   In the United States they exceed two millions and a half, so taking the lead of all other denominations of Christians; and the grand total for the world is not less than three millions.

But this is not the principal sign of growth.   There is a fuller life, a broader sympathy, a larger charity, and a more manifold and wide-spread activity.   Baptist ideas being conceded by the ablest interpreters of Scripture, and the most thorough historians of the Church, we have learnt to be faithful to conscience, without being exclusive ; and to insist on loyalty to Christ,without confound- ing it with loyalty to ourselves.   Colleges have increased in number, and in perfectness of machinery.   Our Literature has grown, though Baptists have yet to learn to appreciate, at its real value, this mighty organ for good.   The BAPTIST UNION has taken shape, and is blending together Baptists of all shades and conditions for the common welfare of the Churches, the good of the nation, and the salvation of the world.   Missions to the heathen embrace new and wider areas, and sedulously till the old fields with a larger hope and an expanding toil.

It is undeniable that Baptist Ideas are alive, and beneficially aggressive, and were never more so since the days of the Apostles.

BAPTISTS; THEIR DISTINCTIVE PRINCIPLES.

BY THE

REV. JOHN BATEY.

———◆———

THE Distinctive Principles of the Baptists admit of a much wider survey than I at first contemplated in the present Lecture. Viewed in distinction from those of the Church of Rome, they include the right of private judgment in all matters of religion, together with the perfect sufficiency of the Word of God as the only rule of faith and practice. In distinction from the Church of England, as by law established, we hold that the religion of Christ "is not of this world," and is therefore absolutely independent of all State control. In distinction from the Society of Friends, we believe in the perpetuity of the Christian Ordinances of Baptism and the Lord's Supper. In distinction from the Presbyterians, the Moravians, and the various bodies of Methodists, we maintain that each separate Church has, within itself, the exclusive right to choose its own Pastors and Office-bearers, to receive and exclude its members, and to manage its own affairs irrespective of all external control. Finally, in distinction from the practice of Pœdobaptists of every name, we hold that the immersion of believers on a profession of repentance toward God, and faith toward our Lord Jesus Christ, is the only baptism that is authorised by the precepts, or sanctioned by the examples, of the New Testament Scriptures.

From the uniform practice of the Apostles, as recorded in the Book which bears their name, as also in their several epistles to the Churches which they planted and governed, it is clear in

c

what light they understood the Commission which they had received from their Lord and Master, to preach the Gospel, and to administer the ordinances of His Kingdom.

The time and circumstances under which their Divine Leader gave them their final instructions are very significant, and should be carefully considered by all who wish to know the place which Baptism occupies in His Kingdom. He had but recently been raised from the dead. Before His death, and just after He had broken bread with the disciples at the celebration of the Passover, He said unto them, " After I am risen again I will go before you into Galilee." On the morning of His resurrection the Angel of the Lord said unto them that were early at the sepulchre, " Go quickly, and tell His disciples that He is risen from the dead ; and, behold, He goeth before you into Galilee ; there shall ye see Him. And as they went to tell His disciples, behold, Jesus met them, saying, All hail." Here then, on one of the mountains of Galilee, He called the eleven disciples unto Him, and said " All power is given unto me in heaven and in earth." It was at this most solemn and interesting moment that He instituted Christian Baptism. If ever it were necessary for the great Teacher to use great plainness of speech, to speak so that He could not be misunderstood, it was at this solemn crisis. He was about to take His final departure from His disciples. He had completed the work which His Father had given Him to do, and was about to enter into that glory, which He had before the world was created. They would not, therefore, have the opportunity of applying to Him personally to settle any dispute which might arise among themselves in the execution of the work which He had called them to perform. It is true, He promised to send them the Holy Spirit to lead them into *all truth*, and to bring all things to their remembrance whatsoever He had said unto them. Accordingly He poured out the Holy Spirit, on the day of Pentecost, and it is owing to His inspirations that we have the infallible teachings of the New Testament Scriptures. But the Holy Spirit was not given to teach the meaning of words which had been employed by the Saviour during His ministry on Earth. It was, according to His promise, to "bring all things to their remembrance, whatsoever He had said unto them." Now, if we can find that the Holy Spirit brought *Infant Baptism* to their remembrance, it will be a decisive proof that Christ had taught them to baptize infants, but if we find that they never, in any single instance even referred to it, then it is impossible that demonstration can be more complete, that it was not instituted by Christ, but that it was, as is admitted by many of the most learned Pædobaptists themselves, introduced into the Church long after the death of the last of the Apostles. This remark applies with equal force both to the *nature and subjects* of baptism.

In the course of the present Lecture I shall have occasion to refer to numerous writers who admit the Scriptural character of the distinctive principles of the Baptists, but only as confirmatory of their validity, and not as the foundation of their authority. "The Bible, and the Bible alone" being the standard of our final appeal in all that we believe and practise on all matters of our religion :—what then, do the Holy Scriptures teach concerning the institution of Christian Baptism ?

I. Its NATURE. I say *nature* rather than *mode*, for the same thing may have several different modes, hence those who are not Baptists say the *mode* of baptism is of little consequence as it may be performed either by dipping, pouring, or sprinkling.

Now, we maintain that *immersion* only is baptism. It would be as proper to say that sprinkling or pouring are modes of dipping as that they are modes of baptism. It is well known that the word "Baptism" is not an English word. It is a Greek word left untranslated. The word "Baptize" in the New Testament, differs only from the Greek word "Baptizo" in the last letter ; E being substituted for o. A most singular method this, certainly, of conveying the meaning of a Greek word to an

English reader. The impropriety of this will appear by considering that if the same method had been adopted by the translators with every other word in the Sacred Scriptures, the Bible would have been to the unlearned a dead letter, and they must have remained for ever in utter ignorance of God and Christ, and the way of salvation. And was it not wrong in the translators, in this way, to conceal the Christian's duty and privilege under a Greek word? They could not be ignorant of the fact that its proper meaning was " *to immerse*," for they have actually translated the word " Bapto" "*to dip*," in several places in the New Testament. " He that *dippeth* his hand with me in the dish," " That Lazarus may *dip* the tip of his finger in water," " He it is to whom I shall give a sop when I have *dipped* it." Let the English reader remember that neither " Bapto " nor " Baptizo " is ever translated "*sprinkle*" or "*pour*" in the New Testament; and that wherever sprinkling or pouring occurs, quite different words are used. Now, would not our Saviour, if He had meant pouring or sprinkling have used these words, and not words which had a totally *opposite* signification? If He had intended His disciples to sprinkle, would He not have used the Greek word " Rhantizo " which signifies " to sprinkle " and not "*Baptizo*" which signifies "to *immerse?*" Is it consistent to suppose that the infinitely wise Jesus would use a word which means " to dip," when He only meant *pouring* or *sprinkling?* Impossible! That the word " Baptizo " ought to have been translated "to dip," "plunge " or "immerse" is capable of the fullest demonstration.

As a matter of fact it is admitted by the most learned Divines that ever lived, that this is its proper signification, although for the sake of *convenience* they *substituted* " sprinkling or pouring." Before I quote these authorities, I will appeal to several classic writers to show that *dipping* is the meaning of the word. These must be admitted to be competent and disinterested witnesses. And let it be borne in mind that what is true of the Sacred Scriptures is equally true of these, that there is not a single instance to be found in all their writings where " *Baptizo* " is used for sprinkling or pouring, but invariably for *dipping, sinking, covering, overwhelming,* or *immersing.*

The word " Baptizo " is used in the following quotations :—

Anacreon. "Taking hold of Cupid by the wings, immersed, or plunged him into the wine."

Æsop. "The dolphin vexed at such a falsehood, immersing him, killed him."

Diodorus Siculus. " Most of the land animals, if they are intercepted by the river, are destroyed, being immersed."

Josephus speaking of the death of Aristobulus, says,—"The young man was sent to Jericho, and there, according to his order, being *immersed* in a fish pond, he came to his end." Again, speaking of one Simon, he says—"Going through all his kindred, and standing conspicuously on their bodies, as if to be concealed from no one, he *plunged* his whole sword into his bowels."

Polybius uses the word " Ebaptizon " when speaking of a sea fight between the Romans and Carthaginians, "They *immersed* or sunk," he says, "many vessels of the Romans."

It is surely unnecessary to multiply instances, although a volume could be produced to the same purpose. These are sufficient both in number and perspicuity to show its literal meaning in classic authors. The force of the argument derived from this source has been felt and acknowledged by many learned Pædobaptists. Dr. Wall, the Pædobaptist historian, tells us that the Greek Church has always used immersion. An authoritative writer, Alexander de Stourzas, says "the word baptizo has but *one* signification, it signifies literally and perpetually, to immerse ; baptism and immersion are identical, and to say baptism by sprinkling is the same as to say immersion by sprinkling, 'or any other contradiction in terms."

I will add to these testimonies, the concessions of some of the most learned and pious divines. And, let it be remembered that they are the statements of men who did not hold our distinctive principle, and that therefore, the evidence in favour of immersion must have been absolutely irresistible. With their consistency or inconsistency I have nothing to do. I shall simply quote their words, and leave others to form their own opinion, but at the same time, would affectionately caution them against following a practice, which their own judgment and consciences tell them is unauthorised by the word of God, the only rule of faith and practice.

> Bishop Bossuet says : "It is *certain* that John the Baptist baptized in no other way than by dipping."
>
> John Calvin says : "The word baptism signifies 'to dip,' and it is *certain* that the manner of dipping was used by the old Church."
>
> Beza says : "Christ commanded us to be baptized, by which it is *certain* immersion is meant."
>
> Martin Luther says : "I could wish that such as are to be baptized should be completely immersed into the water, according to the meaning of the word, and the signification of the ordinance, as also *without doubt* it was instituted by Christ."
>
> James Mede says : "There was no such thing as sprinkling used in the Apostles' days, nor many years after then."
>
> Dr. Whitby says : "Immersion was religiously observed by all Christians for *thirteen centuries*, and was approved by the Church of England. And since the change of it into sprinkling was made without any allowance from the *Author* of the institution, or any license from any Council of the Church, being that which the Romanist still urgeth to justify his refusal of the cup to the laity, it were to be wished that this custom might be again of general use."

Dr. Campbell says : "The word 'baptism,' both in sacred and classical writers, signifies to *dip*, to *plunge*, to *immerse*."

Dr. Chalmers, commenting on Romans vi. 4, 7, says : "The original meaning of the word *baptism* is *immersion*, and though we regard it as a point of indifferency whether the ordinance so named be performed this way or by sprinkling, yet we doubt not that the prevalent style of the administration in the Apostles' days was by the actual submerging of the *whole body* under water. We advert to this for the purpose of throwing light on the analogy which is instituted in these verses. Jesus Christ, by death, underwent this sort of baptism, even immersion under the surface of the ground, whence He soon emerged again by His resurrection. We, by being baptized into His death are conceived to have made a similar translation, in the act of *descending* under the water of baptism to have resigned an old life, and in the act of *ascending* to *emerge* into a second, or new life."

Albert Barnes says : "It is absolutely certain that John immersed. There is not room for even the shadow of a doubt."

Neander says : "The practice of immersion was *beyond doubt* prevalent in the *whole Church.*"

Dean Stanley says : "There can be no doubt that the original form of baptism—the very meaning of the word—was complete immersion in deep waters. *The change from immersion to sprinkling has set aside the apostolic language regarding Baptism and has altered the very meaning of the word.*"

Now the question is, do the Holy Scriptures agree with this signification of the word baptism ? If they teach immersion to be baptism, then it is to be expected that they will *not* speak of a *basin* containing a little water, nor of a Minister putting his

fingers into water, nor of pouring or sprinkling a few drops upon
the heads of either babes or men. On the contrary, if they *dipped*
or *immersed* we may expect to find that they went to a *river*, to
a place where there was "*much water*," that they were "*buried* in
baptism" and that they "*went into the water*." Now, do the Scriptures speak in this way? Let us hear them. "And were all
baptized of him in the river Jordan." "John was baptizing in
Ænon, near to Salim, because there was much water there."
"And they went down both *into* the water, both Philip and the
eunuch; and he baptized him." To suppose these baptisms to
have been sprinklings is preposterous, but if they were immersions, all is beautiful and consistent. The baptism of our Blessed
Lord is recorded in Mark i. 9, "And it came to pass in those
days, that Jesus came from Nazareth of Galilee, and was baptized
of John in Jordan." Dr. Bloomfield, in his Greek Testament with
English notes, gives the following translation : "Literally, *dipped*
or plunged into." How forcible must truth be, thus to compel
a dignitary of the Church of England so to translate the word of
God as to prove that those who pour or sprinkle for baptism,
depart from the precept and example of the Lord Jesus Christ.
We may ask again, do the sacred writers ever allude to baptism
in such forms of expression as imply that immersion and not
sprinkling is the very nature of the ordinance? The words of
the Apostle, Roman vi. 3-4, give a decisive answer : "Know
ye not that so many of us as were baptized into Jesus Christ were
baptized into His death? Therefore we are *buried* with Him by
baptism into death." Now what is *burial?* That we may have an
unbiased answer let Dr. Johnson give it : "Burial—the act of placing
under earth and water." Now baptism is of course the placing of
the candidate *under water*. This testimony to the Scripture nature
of baptism, though undesigned at the time by the Prince of lexi-
cographers, is worth a volume of the hard pleading of Ewing,
Wardlaw, and Beecher   That this passage alludes to immersion is
admitted by some of the best and most learned Pædobaptists.

Bishop Burnet asserts : " We know that the first ritual of baptism was by going into the waters, and being laid as dead backwards all along in them, and then the persons baptized were raised up again, and so they came out of them.   This is not only mentioned by St. Paul, but in two different places he gives a mystical signification of this rite, that it signified our being buried with Christ in baptism, and our being raised up again to a new life."

Archbishop Tillotson says ; " Anciently, those who were baptized were immersed, and buried in the water."

Dr. McKnight says : " The baptized person is buried under the water."

Dr. Doddridge remarks : " It seems the part of candour to confess that here is an allusion to the manner of baptizing by immersion."

George Whitfield observes : " It is certain that in these words there is an allusion to the manner of baptism which was by immersion."

Dr. Barth remarks : " The expression appears particularly appropriate when we recollect the custom prevalent at the time of immersing the whole body in baptism."

What need have we of further witness ?   When will the Church of Christ be consistent ? " To the law and to the testimony, if they speak not according to this word, it is because there is no light in them."

It may be deemed necessary here to notice a few objections which have been raised against immersion.   This I shall gladly do for the sake of those who have been kept from embracing the Scripture view of the subject, by the mists which have been thrown around it from false principles of criticism and supposed expediency.   The Greek word " *Baptizo* " it is said is only a derivative from " Bapto," and therefore a *diminutive*.   Now this is contrary to the opinion of one of the most profound Greek scholars that ever lived. " Not long before the death of Professor Porson," says Dr. Newman, " I went, in company with a much respected friend, to see that celebrated Greek scholar at the London Institution. I was curious to hear how he read Greek. He very condescendingly at my request, took down a Greek Testament and read perhaps twenty verses from one of the Gospels, in which the word ' Bapto ' occurred. I said, ' Sir, you know there is a controversy among Christians respecting the meaning of that word.' He smiled and replied, ' The Baptists have the advantage of us.' He cited immediately the well known passage in Pindar, and one or two of those in the Gospels mentioned in this letter. I enquired whether in his opinion ' *Baptizo* ' must be considered equal to ' *Bapto*,' which he said was ' to tinge ' as dyers ; he replied to this effect, ' That if there be a difference he should take the former to be the strongest.' He fully assured me that it signified a total immersion." In this learned professor's opinion " *Baptizo*," although a derivative is not a diminutive, but like its root " Bapto " signifies " *to dip ;* " and what is remarkable, while " Bapto " is used in a *secondary* sense " *to dye*," " Baptizo " is never used with any other signification than to immerse. This fully corroborates the opinion of the late Dr. Carson.

Another objection has been raised on the supposed indeterminate nature of Greek prepositions. It is said *eis* (into), and *ek* (out of), may be rendered *to* and *from*. What then, does it imply that they went to *rivers* and places where there was " *much water* " to sprinkle ? Do those who sprinkle go to rivers now ? What would be thought of a Wesleyan or a Congregationalist going to the river Thames, or to the Serpentine in Hyde Park, to sprinkle any number of persons ? That *into* is the true meaning of *eis* will appear from the following texts : " Enter *into* thy closet ; " " A net cast *into* the sea ; " " He falleth *into* the fire and *into* the water ; " " Carried up *into* heaven." The absurdity of raising an objection to immersion because *eis* may be rendered " to " or " at " must appear to every one. Besides, the narrative of the Baptism of the Eunuch puts it beyond all doubt that *into* is the only proper rendering, in connection with baptism. Luke tells us that as Philip and the Eunuch "went on their way and came unto a certain water," and then "they went *down* both *into* the water." If this does not prove that they went *into* the water, it would be impossible to find words to convey such an idea.

Another objection is founded on 1 Corinthians x. 2, where it is said that "the Israelites were baptised unto Moses in the cloud and in the sea." But this agrees much better with immersion than sprinkling. The Israelites resembled persons immersed or buried. Moses says : they "went into the midst of the sea upon the dry ground, and the waters were a wall unto them on their right hand and on their left," while the cloud literally *covered* them. This was, therefore, a complete though figurative immersion. So it was regarded by Dean Alford, who says they " entered by the act of such immersion into a solemn covenant with God."

Again it is objected that the washing of cups, pots, beds, &c., is inconsistent with immersion, but that eminent and learned Jewish commentator, Rabbi Maimonides, says : " Every vessel of wood, as a table or bed, receives defilement, and these were washed by *covering* in *water*, and very nice and particular they were that they might be covered all over." Again, " If the Pharisees touched but the garments of the common people, they were defiled all over as if they had touched a dead person and needed *immersion*, and were obliged to do it." Dr. Bloomfield, in his " Greek Testament with English notes," says : " Wash themselves, that is, their *bodies*, as opposed to the washing of the hands only.'' Now, this, so far from being in favour of sprinkling, is an irrefutable argument for immersion.

Another objection is founded on the " divers washings " (*baptisms*) mentioned, Heb. ix. 10. The most unwarrantable inference has been drawn from this verse. It has been said that

the apostle alludes to washings by sprinklings ! But where is
the proof ? There is none. But there is the reverse. We have
the true key to the "divers baptisms," Num. xix. 7 : "Then
the Priest shall wash his *clothes*, and he shall *bathe* his flesh *in*
water." By comparing this passage with others of a similar import, in other parts of the writings of Moses, it will be clearly
seen that St. Paul is not referring at all to the sprinkling of blood,
but to *divers immersions* in water.

Others, again, object that there was not sufficient water, and
that it was impossible to immerse three thousand on the day of
Pentecost ! If this were a fact, of course the question would be
settled in favour of sprinkling. But is it a fact ? We maintain
not. It is well known that Jerusalem was well supplied with
reservoirs, besides immense pools and fountains abounding with
water. This is testified by many travellers. Dr. Robinson says :
" There are, on the North side of the city, outside of the walls,
two very large reservoirs, one of which is 300 feet long, and more
than 200 feet wide ; and the other over 600 feet long by over 250
wide." Inside the walls, he mentions the pool of Bathsheba, the
pool of Bethesda, and the pool of Hezekiah, all being several
hundred feet in length and breadth, besides which, he refers to
numerous fountains. As to the 3,000, it is not said that they were
all baptised on the day of Pentecost, or that they were all baptized by the Apostles. Many of the seventy other disciples might
baptize, so that there would be time enough and to spare.

The last objection I shall name is founded on the Baptism of
the Holy Spirit. That must be a poor cause that takes refuge in
a figure of speech. But even this proves that immersion, and not
sprinkling or pouring, is baptism. The celebrated Dr. Campbell,
though a Pædobaptist, renders the words of John, " He will baptize *in* the Holy Spirit and fire." And there is nothing absurd in
speaking of being immersed in the Holy Spirit. We speak of
being immersed in debt or in trouble. But it is said that the
Holy Spirit was *poured* out. True, but it is not said the *pouring*

was the *baptism*. The water is often poured into our baptistries, but will it be said we therefore baptize by *pouring* ? It was when He *was poured* out that they were immersed in the Holy Spirit. That eminent Greek Professor, J. Casaubon, says : "Regard is had in this place (Acts i. 5) to the proper signification of the word baptism, to immerse, or dip ; and in this sense the Apostles are truly said to be baptized, for the house was filled with the Holy Ghost, so that the Apostles seemed to be plunged into it as into some pool."

Having proved, as I believe, that immersion only, is baptism, and answered the most plausible objections against it, I proceed to consider

II.—THE SUBJECTS OF CHRISTIAN BAPTISM.—It is well known that the *subject* is as much contested as the *nature*. As I am reasoning with Protestants, and not with Romanists, it must be borne in mind that my standard of ultimate appeal will be to the written word of God. "If any man speak, let him speak as the oracles of God." Our inquiry must not be, "What saith the Church ?" but "What saith the Lord ?" Now, the Lord has spoken, and spoken so explicitly and definitely, that it is impossible for us to mistake, if we are only prepared to take His word and let that decide the controversy. This distinctive principle of our Protestant faith is forcibly put by Dr. Chalmers. "The Bible," he says, "will allow of no compromise. It professes to be the directory of our faith, and claims a total ascendency over the souls and the understandings of men. It will enter into no composition with us, or our natural principles. It challenges the whole mind as its due, and it appeals to the truth of heaven for the high authority of its sanctions. Whoever addeth to, or taketh from, the words of this book, is accursed, is the absolute language in which it delivers itself. This brings us to its terms. There is no way of escaping this. We must bring every thought into the captivity of its obedience, and closely as ever lawyer stuck to his document or to his extract, must we abide by the rule and the doctrine which this authentic memorial of God sets before us."

Now we will first refer to the Commission of Christ respecting Baptism. It reads: "Go ye therefore, and teach all nations, baptizing them in the name of the Father, and of the Son, and of the Holy Ghost." So Matthew. It is equally explicit in Mark, and by its very terms excludes infants. "Go ye," said the Saviour, "into all the world, and preach the Gospel to every creature ; he that believeth and is baptized shall be saved." These words so positively restrict baptism to *believers*, that many of the most pious and learned Pædobaptists have admitted it. Baxter says : "This is not like some occasional, historical mention of baptism, but it is the very Commission of Christ to his Apostles, for preaching and baptizing, and purposely expresseth their several *places* and *order*. Their first task is by *teaching* to make *disciples*, which are, by Mark, called *believers ;* the *second* work is to baptize them, whereto is annexed their salvation ; the *third* work is to teach them all things, which are afterwards to be learned in the school of Christ. To contemn *this order* is to *renounce* all rules of order ; for where can we expect to find it if not here ? I profess my conscience is fully satisfied from this text, that it is one sort of faith, even saving, that must go before baptism, and the profession whereof, the minister must expect." Dr. Dwight says, "Here they were to make disciples of mankind first, and then baptize them, and thus to seal their discipleship." It is certain therefore that if infant baptism be scriptural, it cannot be proved by this commission. This *excludes* them, whatever else may *include* them. It would be as easy to establish the baptism of *idiots*, or even *bells*, as the baptism of infants from this commission. It is "he that *believeth* and is baptized shall be saved." The command of St. Peter on the day of Pentecost to those who inquired what they must do to be saved, may be regarded as a correct application of the commission. "Repent," said he, "and be baptized every one of you in the name of Jesus Christ for the remission of sins, and ye shall receive the gift of the Holy Ghost."

Look in the next place to the examples of baptisms as recorded in the New Testament. Here again, strange as it may appear to some, there is the most absolute silence in regard to the baptism of infants. There is not one single instance of the baptism of a child. This is freely admitted by many Pædobaptists. Dr. Wall confesses, "Among all the persons that are recorded as baptized by the Apostles, there is no express mention of an infant." Calvin says, "It is nowhere expressed by the Evangelists that *any one infant* was baptized." T. Boston says, "There is no example of baptism recorded in the Scriptures where any were baptized but such as appeared to have a saving interest in Christ." Dr. Paley says, "At the time the Scriptures were written *none* were baptized but *converts.*" Dr. Goodwin says, "Read all the Acts, still it is said, they believed and were baptized." Olshausen remarks, "There is altogether wanting any conclusive proof for the baptism of children in the age of the Apostles." Hence, if there is nothing in the Commission of Christ respecting the baptism of infants, and if there is no, instance in Scripture of the Apostles baptizing infants, then it must be clear that infant baptism is a human invention. If it is *not in* the Scriptures, it cannot be scriptural. Consequently, it is a tradition of men, and altogether without the highest authority in the service of Christ. The very nature of His religion proves that infants are unfit subjects of baptism. It is entirely personal and voluntary. No commandment of Christ can be obeyed by proxy. Parents are not commanded to have their children baptized, as they were, under the law, to have them circumcised. The duty is personal. "*He* that believeth and is baptized." "Repent and be baptized *every one* of you." Faith and repentance are not more personal than is baptism. The great Teacher says, "Whosoever does not bear his cross, and come after me, cannot be my disciple." We are first to be made *disciples;* and then, and not till then, baptized. "Jesus *made* and *baptized* more disciples than John."

That infants are not proper subjects of baptism is evident from the *symbolical* import of the ordinance. It clearly represents our death unto sin, and our new birth unto righteousness. "Know ye not that so many of us as were baptized into Jesus Christ were baptized into his death? therefore we are buried with Him by baptism unto death : that like as Christ was raised up from the dead, by the glory of the Father, even so we also should walk in newness of life." Now, are infants baptized into Jesus Christ? Are they baptized into His death? Do they die to sin? Do they rise from the dead into a new life? We know they do not. Do they put on Christ? Certainly not. But the Apostle declares, that "as many of you as have been baptized into Christ *have put on Christ.*" It appears plain also from the command to *teach* the baptized, that infants are not its legitimate subjects. Our Lord says in the Commission, " Teaching them to observe all things whatsoever I have commanded you." Now, can you teach infants these things as soon as they are baptized? If you cannot, then it is evident, they are not to be baptized. It is vain to say that they can be taught after they grow up, for the command is connected with *baptism*, and the *teaching* therefore is *immediately* to follow. In this ordinance a profession of faith in Christ is made before men. But, can infants profess faith which they do not possess? They cannot even *seem* to have faith ; Their baptism therefore is utterly without meaning. The Church of Rome, and after her the Church of England, seeing this, have invented an order of sponsors, or sureties, called godfathers and godmothers, who solemnly promise that they will renounce the Devil and all his works and follow a life of piety ; and this, while it is well known that the persons very frequently have no faith, and no religion, and are in fact sometimes persons of immoral character. Then, when the children are arrived at a certain age, they are what they call *confirmed*, and are made to say that in their baptism they were " made members of Christ, children of God, and inheritors of the kingdom of heaven." It is thought by some that the words of

Christ, "Suffer little children, and forbid them not, to come unto me; for of such is the kingdom of heaven," is a sufficient warrant for the baptizing of infants. But this text is more against it than for it. It does not say one word about their baptism. The children were not brought to Christ to be baptized, but to be blessed. It will as much prove that children ought to be brought to the Lord's table as to baptism. Neither does the text say that little children are in the kingdom of heaven, but that, as Mr. Barnes says, "Of *such* as these, that is, of persons with such tempers as these, is the church to be composed. He does not say *of those infants*, but of such as resemble them." This is put in its true light by the Saviour when He says, "except ye be converted and become *as* little children, ye shall not enter into the kingdom of heaven." What the passage proves is this, that children may be brought to Christ to receive His blessing. It lays a sufficient foundation for their *salvation*, but none for their *baptism*.

Others have found a reason for infant baptism in 1 Cor. vii. 14, "For the unbelieving husband is sanctified by the wife, and the unbelieving wife is sanctified by the husband, else were your children unclean; but now are they holy." Now, whatever may be the meaning of the terms "holy" and "unclean" in this text, it is clear that it proves too much to be of any service in the argument. For if the children were to be baptized because in some sense they were holy, then the unbelieving husband, and the unbelieving wife, were equally eligible, for each was *sanctified*, by the believing partner. Even Dean Stanley says that "the passage on the one hand is *against* the practice of infant baptism in the Apostles' time," although, he imagined "on the other hand, it contained the principle on which it is founded." H. J. Gamble says, "I am not prepared to urge it in favour of infant baptism." The practice of circumcision in the Jewish Church is considered by many a sufficient ground for infant baptism in the Christian Church. It ought to be a sufficient reply to this that it is never so said in the word of God. It is a mere assumption. Why ! if baptism came in the place of circumcision, then only male children should be baptized. But Dr. Halley, the champion of infant baptism, has conclusively proved, in opposition to his brethren, that the law of circumcision is no warrant for the baptism of a child. He remarks, "The *Jewish* parent transmitted the *natural relation* to his child, and, of course transmitted its *privileges*, but the *Christian* does not transmit the *spiritual* relation, and therefore, does not transmit its *privileges.*"

The baptism of households is considered by many an unanswerable argument in proof of the baptism of infants. Now, if it could be shown that there were infants in the three households which are named, then there might be a presumption in favour of their baptism. But can this be proved ? By no means. That there *were not* is clearly implied. As it regards Lydia, it is not even known that she was a married woman, and those of her household are called " *brethren.*" As to the Jailer's family, the Apostles Paul and Silas preached the gospel *to all* that were in his house, and when he and all his were baptized, he rejoiced, believing in God with all his house. "Here was a *hearing*, a *believing*, a *baptized*, and a *rejoicing* household." The members of the household of Stephanas were the first fruits of the gospel in Achaia, who "addicted themselves to the ministry of the saints." Any Baptist minister would be glad to baptize such households as these, and *many such have been baptized.* St. John mentions a nobleman, who *himself* believed, and his *whole* house.

Some plead Acts ii. 39, " The promise is unto you and to your children, and to all that are afar off, even as many as the Lord our God shall call." But it is certain, the " children " mentioned in this text are not *infants* but *descendants* according to Acts iii. 35, " Ye are the children of the prophets." Besides it was the *promise* and not *baptism*, and *that* is limited to " *as many* as the Lord our God *shall call.*" But, now it is shown that there is no authority in the New Testament for infant baptism, some will be ready to plead its *Antiquity*. But is it consistent for Protestants to argue in this way ? It is the very argument by which a Romanist would prove all his dogmas. But alas ! as old as infant baptism is, it cannot be traced to the days of the Apostles. *It is extremely doubtful whether it is even named for two hundred years after Christ.* Referring to the latter part of the Apostolic age, Neander, the great church historian, says, "It is in the highest degree probable that the practice of infant baptism was *unknown at this period.*" Then remember, that *infant fellowship* at the Lord's table can be traced as far back on the pages of history as infant baptism ! They must stand or fall together ! Infants are as fit for one as for the other. If faith is required for communion, so it is for baptism. "He that believeth and is baptized shall be saved." This is Christ's own law of baptism. The distinctive principles of Baptists will not allow us to alter His law. That all who *die* in infancy are *saved* we *rejoice* to *believe*. "They *die*, for Adam sinned : they *live*, for Jesus died," for "He died for all."

Our distinctive principles save us from the pernicious errors of baptismal regeneration and sacramental grace. Our practice in regard to baptism is an explicit and perpetual testimony to the reality of our Saviour's death and resurrection, and, by consequence, to the truth and divine origin of the Christian religion. Herein we show forth His *death* and *resurrection* "till He come," who "being made perfect, became the Author of eternal salvation unto all them that *obey* Him. To Him be glory and dominion for ever and ever. Amen."

BAPTIST MARTYRS.

BY

W. J. AVERY.

A MARTYR is a witness. That is the primary and essential meaning of the term. But it is applied more especially to those who witness for the truth of their *convictions*. And its signification is still further restricted by reference to those only who *suffer death* for conscience sake, whilst comparatively few lay claim to it, save those who perish in the behalf of the *Christian* Faith. To this elect body, Baptist confessors undoubtedly belong. They have *witnessed*—witnessed for *principles* —for the principles of the *Christian* religion---and have shown themselves "faithful unto *death*" in the testimony they bore.

"The noble army" of Baptist Martyrs is so vast that only a selection of names can be made for the present purpose. If, however, the first available name were not to be mentioned, a most illustrious association would be ignored, and we should practically deny our historic interest in that brave champion for righteousness concerning whom our Lord Himself affirmed—"Among them that are born of women there hath not risen a greater than John the Baptist." He was emphatically a witness of Christ, and the terms of his testimony are ever before us—"Behold the Lamb of God." He it was through whom his Master, in example and in precept, instituted that ordinance by which Baptists are chiefly distinguished. "Thus it becometh us to fulfil all righteousness." Significant motto that, for those who bear the Baptist name! Would that it were adopted amongst us in all things unto the perfect obedience of His law, who is "The Truth." And was it not this strict fidelity that made John the Baptist a martyr? "*Fulfil all* righteousness." That is the teaching echoing and re-echoing in all his ministry, until at length, in the face of Herod's corrupt court, that denunciation rings out which brings down the wrath of Herodias, and the speedy execution of the prophet. First of all martyrs since the Advent of the Messiah, may not we Baptists, for the best of reasons, place his name upon our roll ?

We need do no more than glance at the great names of the early Christian Church, to recognize in them a strong support to the Faith we profess. "With only one known exception," for the first, second, and third centuries of the Christian era, all Christian martyrs were *Baptists.* The exception was "Cyprian of Carthage," who has been styled "the father of pædo-baptism." He "was a man of God, and a martyr;" but even he "did not plead any law of Christ, or Apostolical tradition for infant baptism." He and his clergy "put the whole thing upon analogy and inference,—upon the necessity of infants on the one hand, and the unlimited grace of God on the other." They did not so much as assert a *belief* for the foundation of their practice, but merely stated what was their "*opinion.*"

In A.D. 251, The Novatians, who assumed the names of Cathari (Puritani), or Pure Churches, separated from the so-called Catholic Church. These Churches held the Catholics to have so far departed from the principle of pure membership, communion, and discipline, that they regarded "the baptism administered by so corrupt a Church as null and void." Hence they baptized all who joined them from the Catholics, and so are the first in history who were called *Anabaptists*, that is, *re-baptizers.*

When Constantine came into power, it is estimated there had been three millions of Christian martyrs, and these, with the solitary exception of Cyprian, however much they might have departed from the truth in other respects, held faithfully to the doctrine of Baptism as taught by Jesus Christ.

In the fifth century, the Novatians, having previously refused incorporation with the Roman Catholic Imperial Church, set themselves resolutely against the practice of infant baptism. The writings of Augustine had given a stimulus to that innovation upon primitive ritual, and Augustine himself presided over the Council of Carthage, of which the following is one of the canons : " We will that whosoever denies that little children by baptism are freed from perdition and eternally saved, that they be accursed." " From this influence came also, the edict of Honorius and Valentinian III. (A.D. 413) forbidding re-baptism (as it was termed) under the penalty of death . . . From this time, therefore, *the Pure Churches,* became the victims of perpetual persecutions from the hands of the Roman Catholics."

But I have cited enough to show that Believers' Baptism is a doctrine which has been tested not only in the martyrdoms of the Middle Ages and of Reformation times, but also in those of the first five centuries of Christian history. It will be more interesting to know of men and women, who, in later times, forfeited their lives in refusing to yield principles which we also declare and defend.

I. By far the greater number of Baptist Martyrs *suffered on the Continent,* or at least, more persons *known as Baptists* have suffered there than in England. But everywhere, observes Dr. Underhill, in the introduction to " Baptist Martyrology," page v., " by common consent Baptists are excluded from the category of martyrs ; or if perchance a stray name be inscribed in the registers of the reformed, the religious belief of the honored individual is carefully concealed on those points that were obnoxious to the orthodoxy established by Luther, Zwingle, or Calvin." This statement is confirmed by an American writer, as follows : " Good old ' Father Foxe ' in his ' Actes and Monuments,' conceals, where he can, the views of our fathers on their peculiarities ; and when he cannot do this, he labors to extenuate and excuse what the good old man personally considered 'the errors of the Anabaptists.'

Still, however, the facts are sometimes developed, even by himself, and in other instances by contemporary writers; so that no small difficulty presents itself in making a selection from the great number of those who died not only for the Gospel, but also to keep in the Church 'the ordinances as they were delivered.'"

1.—ARNOLD OF BRESCIA

appeared about A.D. 1137 and became "a powerful opponent to the Church of Rome." Having studied in early life under the renowned Peter Abelard, "he returned into Italy, assumed the habit of a monk, and began to propagate his opinions in the streets of Brescia, where he soon gained attention. He especially directed his zeal against the wealth and luxury of the Roman clergy," and consequently, was condemned in an ecclesiastical Council "to perpetual silence." He next went to Zurich, but it was soon necessary for him to leave the canton because of the opposing influence of the famous Bernard of Clairvaux—the author of several of our sweetest hymns, *e.g.*, that commencing "Jesus, the very thought of Thee." "The bold man now conceived the plan and hazarded the desperate experiment of visiting Rome, and fixing the standard of reform in the very heart of the capital." For a while he appeared to succeed, but "at length, in 1155, the Pope laid an interdict on the city. As the sword was no weapon in Arnold's panoply the noble champion retired to Tuscany. There he was seized, brought back to Rome, condemned, crucified, and burnt. His ashes were thrown into the Tiber." In the sketch given of his career it is added, "Many very decisive facts show Arnold to have been a Baptist. Bernard accuses his followers of mocking at infant baptism. And, Arnold himself was formally condemned by the Lateran Council for rejecting infant baptism." Moreover, his followers (whom Bernard accused as we have seen)—"the Arnoldists—are often met with in ecclesiastical history as a body who were worthy of his name, and of our high respect," and concerning them, "Evervinus, in Germany,

says, 'the Arnoldists condemn the (Catholic) sacraments, particularly baptism, which they administer only to the adult ; alleging
that place, whoever shall believe and be baptised shall be saved.'"
Truly here is a bright light in the dark days of Rome's apostacy
and ignorance.   Arnold testified seven hundred years ago to the
very truths distinctively taught to-day by our brethren Wall,
Grassi, and Shaw, in that same old city !

2.—FELIX MANTZ

was "a leader in the Reformation in Germany."   Born in Zurich,
he "was educated in all the learning of the age, his father being
a canon of the great minster " of his native city.   In 1519 he was
"studying the Hebrew language with Zwingle, under the tuition
of Carlstadt," and about the year 1522 he began to doubt the
scripturalness of infant baptism.   At first he and Zwingle held
friendly discussion upon the subject, but at length they separated,
and finally Mantz adopted Baptist principles.   In 1523 he began to
preach accordingly, and to insist upon the Church of God being
composed only of believers.   Zwingle says of him--"He wished
to form a church free from sin."   He was imprisoned in March,
1525, but escaped, and proceeded to declare his principles in
various parts of Switzerland.   "He was baptized by Blaurock, a
companion in suffering," and forthwith seized every opportunity
of preaching the gospel in the open air.   Having, however, been
previously prohibited by the magistrates of Zurich from doing this
work, "he was deemed a rebel against legitimate authority and an
exciter of the people to sedition.

"Towards the end of 1526 he was seized and imprisoned in the
tower of Wellenberg.   He confessed that he had baptized contrary
to the edict.   It was right, he said, to obey God rather than man.
Exhibiting no sign of repentance, he was at last adjudged, and on
January 5, 1527, was drowned.

"Bullinger thus writes, 'As he came down from the Wellenberg
to the fishmarket, and was led through the shambles to the boat,

he praised God that he was about to die for His truth ; for ana-baptism was right, and founded on the word of God, and Christ had foretold that His followers would suffer for the truth's sake. And the like discourse he urged much, contradicting the preacher who attended him.   On the way, his mother and brother came to him, and exhorted him to be steadfast ; and he persevered in his folly, even to the end.   When he was bound upon the hurdle, and was about to be thrown into the stream by the executioner, he sung with a loud voice, " Into thy hands, O Lord, I commend my spirit."   And herewith was he drawn into the water by the executioner and drowned.   His body was then taken to the Place and buried at St. Jacob's.'   ' It is reported here,' says Capito, writing to Zwingle, near the end of the same month, ' that your Felix Mantz hath suffered punishment, and died gloriously ; by which the cause of truth and piety, which you sustain, is weighed down exceedingly.' "

Significant words those of Bullinger—" he persevered in his folly even to the end."   Brave Felix Mantz !   Thine was indeed an apostolic spirit.   Like thy predecessor, the Great Teacher of the Gentiles, thou didst not shun to preach the doctrine that was " foolishness to those who were perishing," for thou didst know right well that " the foolishness of God is wiser than men ; and the weakness of God is stronger than men."   It was thine to be chosen of God to confound the wise who charged thee with folly, for the Eternal Wisdom has been manifested in thee, demonstrating to us at this later time, thy godly strength and Christian heroism !

3.—SICKE SNYDER, OR FREERKS.

Early in the sixteenth century a reward was offered for the apprehension of any Baptist preachers found in the Netherlands, and the authorities forbade the harboring of them.   Those who had been rebaptized were ordered to recant, and mercy would be shown to them, " but the obstinate were to be punished with the utmost severity."

At this time there was a faithful follower of Christ bearing the name of Sicke Freerks—a 'Snyder,' or tailor by trade, and hence called Sicke Snyder—who, soon after the edict was published, left the Romish Church, and, determined to obey Christ as his King in all things, was baptized upon confession of his faith. He was consequently imprisoned at Leeuwarden in Friesland, and "endured much suffering from the adversaries of the truth. And, as he could not, by the torments he sustained, be persuaded to apostatize he was there put to death by the sword, displaying great firmness in testifying to the truth, and showing its power on his soul by the manner of his death. His sentence is thus recorded in the criminal sentence-book of the court of Friesland :—'Sicke Freerks, on this 20th of March, 1531, is condemned by the court to be executed with the sword, his body shall be laid on the wheel, and his head set upon a stake, because he has been rebaptized, and perseveres in that baptism.'"

It is particularly interesting to learn the effect of this martyrdom upon Menno Simon, a man who afterwards became "zealous for God, and one of the most eminent teachers and elders." Menno himself says, "It now happened, that I heard from some brethren that a God-fearing pious man, Sicke Snyder by name, had been beheaded at Leeuwarden, because he had renewed his baptism. This sounded wonderfully in my ears, that any should speak of another baptism. I searched the Scriptures with diligence, and reflected earnestly upon them, but could find no trace of infant baptism."

To us, the unscriptural character of infant baptism seems so obvious, that is hard to understand why the emphatic witness of a martyrdom should be needed to rouse anyone to consideration of the matter. And yet one only need remember how hard-beaten the track of superstitious dogma had become, to see the necessity for a demonstrative presentation—a tragic representation—of the truth, such as could be given only in resistance "unto blood." Freerks did not perhaps make a single convert in his life-time, but, in his death, he brought Menno Simon to Jesus, and, "Menno Simon drew great multitudes from the darkness and errors of popery, and from dumb idols to the living God, who were converted and won for God." Thus is individual influence multiplied for the kingdom of light, as abundantly as for the kingdom of darkness.

4, 5.—FYE AND EELKEN

were apprehended about three weeks before the Easter of 1549 in the town of Olde Boor, West Friesland. They were excellent men, and when brought before the magistrates, boldly confessed their faith. Eelken was asked, *inter alia*, if he had been baptized and he replied, "I have not been baptized; but I earnestly desire to be." Both he and Fye received sentence, and so evident was their affection the one for the other, that "the capuchin friars and servants ran and said to the magistrates, 'Never did persons love each other like these.'" Elken said to Fye, "Dear brother, do not reproach me for having been the occasion of your being brought into suffering." Fye's answer was, "Dear brother, do not think that: for it is the power of God."

Eelken was executed first, by the sword. Fye was tempted in the confessional with the bread and wine of the sacrament, but, refusing to partake of them, he affirmed that food was prepared for him in heaven, whereupon "the constable said, 'I have in my life seen many a heretic; but never a more obstinate one than this.'"

Have we not here, harshly named, the quality with which martyrs are signally constituted? Enmity brands it as "obstinacy," but in the estimation of our King it represents the fulfilment of His charge, "Be thou faithful unto death." It is very noticeable in our present review how often this term "obstinate" is reproachfully applied to martyrs. As though they could be excused for having had convictions at variance with ecclesiastical authority, but could have no quarter if they persistently adhered to their beliefs! Such is the irrational tendency of the persecuting spirit.

Fye was strangled, and then burnt. His firmness did not forsake him right through. Without that, mere effusive earnestness will avail but little. This man being constant, everybody could discern his sincerity, insomuch that "the common people cried out, 'That was a pious man! If he was not a Christian, there is not one in the whole world.'"

6.—JAQUES DOSIE

was a youth of fifteen years of age, who, about A.D. 1560 was apprehended at Leeuwarden "for the sake of the truth of the gospel." The Governor's lady took a deep interest in him, and besought him to repent of his baptism, for the sake of life and liberty. "He could by no means be brought to deny Christ; and so was condemned by rulers of the darkness of earth to pass from life to death. He witnessed a good confession in life before many witnesses, and proved the sincerity of his faith in the truth by suffering a bloody and cruel death; thus obtaining the crown of martyrdom, and by the infinite grace of God, we doubt not, the crown of everlasting glory."

7, 8.—STEVEN DE GRAET AND SYNTGEN.

The following is a brief account given by Van Braght—"In the year 1564 was likewise apprehended, at Ghent, in Flanders, for the truth's sake, a brother named Steven de Graet, with Syntgen his aged mother. They were both strong in faith, and persevered therein amidst all temptations and sufferings, even unto death, which they were called to suffer publicly for the name of Christ. They shall also publicly praise the Lord above, before the heavenly throne, and help sing the joyful and new song to the honor of the Lamb, and of Him that sitteth on the throne."

But there is no need to multiply instances of martyrdom

in the ranks of Continental Baptists. "The time would fail
me to tell of" Jerome of Prague, George Wagner of Emmerick,
Leonhard Keyser, Hans of Overdam, and a host of others whose
record is to be found in the pages of "Baptist Martyrology."
Enough has been cited to show that no age, or class, escaped persecution in those times of established intolerance. The young
and the old, the cultured and the ignorant, the wealthy and the
destitute, alike fell before the destroyer. The offence for which
they were in common adjudged to death was the intelligent and
devout observance of baptism by immersion, whereby they ignored
the spurious rite administered by the Church in their infancy.

II.—*Baptist Martyrs in England.*—Near the middle of
the twelfth century, about thirty men and women appeared
at Oxford, who were called *Publicans*—a name supposed to
be a corruption of "Paulicians." They were thorough
Baptists, of eminent spirituality, and by the singularity of their
religious opinions and practices, they soon attracted the attention
of the government. "William of Newbury, a monkish historian,
tells us that these persons, whom he calls vagabonds, emigrated
from Gascony, and spread their doctrine into many regions." He
roundly abuses them for their fidelity to conviction as well as for
the simplicity of their manners—abuse we may observe, not more
reasonable in the one case than in the other. A man may as well
be blamed for wearing a plain coat, as for holding to the plain
truth. "Their pastor named

1.—GERARD

was, it is said, the only person of any learning among them, and
to him they all looked up, as their prince and preceptor."

Henry II. being informed of them, would not allow them to
be punished without a hearing, hence they were arraigned before
a council of Popish bishops at Oxford. Gerard answered for himself and his friends. They denied infant baptism and everything
contrary to the Word of God. "The bishops reported them to

the King as obstinate heretics, worthy of death ; and he, under
priestly influence, sentenced them all to be branded with a red
hot iron on their foreheads, as heretics ; that then they should be
publicly whipped through the streets of Oxford, and be afterwards
delivered to the secular power for further punishment, or, in
other words, should be put to death. . . . . The sentence
was fully carried into execution. Gerard, to distinguish him
from the rest, had a mark burnt on his chin as well as on his fore-
head, and, in the depth of winter, when the hedges and the fields
were covered with snow, every man, woman, and child, was cast
into the fields, almost naked, and the whole of them perished with
cold and hunger. . . . They went forth to endure death, 'not
with lingering steps, but actually rejoicing with much joy ; while
their master preceded them, and sang, Blessed are ye when all
men shall hate you.' "

This was at the time when Thomas à Becket was at the height
of his prosperity. Within the next ten years, he also became a
martyr. But what a contrast between his martyrdom in defence
of the monstrous usurpations of the church, and the witness of
these humble disciples, to the simple truths of the Gospel. Verily,
they shine by the comparison !

The first *Englishman* burnt as a heretic, and for religion only,
was

2.—WILLIAM SAWTRY,

who suffered martyrdom in London, A.D. 1400. Concerning him,
Crosby, the Baptist historian thus writes : Sawtry "had been
sometime minister of the parish of St. Margaret, in the town of
Lynn ; but having entertained the opinions of the Lollards, was
first convicted of heresy by the bishop of Norwich, and afterwards
brought to make a public recantation of the same, and so escaped
for that time ; but coming to London, and retaining still a zeal
for the true religion, he petitioned the parliament that he might
be heard in some matters relating to religion, which he believed

would be for the benefit of the whole kingdom. The clergy sus-
pecting his design, which must have been to get the established
religion reformed, or a toleration for such as dissented, got the
matter to be referred wholly to them in convocation ; who soon
condemned him as an obstinate heretic, and procured a decree
from the king for his burning.

"This proto-martyr of the English nation is thought by some
to have been a Baptist'; because the Lollards, who lived in the
diocese of Norwich, where this man first received and professed
his notions, were generally of that opinion ; and Mr. Foxe, in
relating the errors of which he (Sawtry) was accused by the
Papists, uses the same partiality that he had done before in Wick-
liff's case ; for out of the ten errors of which he was convicted by
the Bishop of Norwich, he conceals the two last, as may be seen
in the scroll and recantation."

As it may be asked why the Lollards of *Norfolk* more especially
held the opinions of the Baptists, it will be as well to remind
ourselves that at an early date those opinions extensively prevailed upon the Continent, particularly in the Netherlands ; that
the counties of Norfolk and Suffolk from their geographical
position afforded a good point of arrival for settlers and refugees
(from persecution and other causes) ; and, in all probability, it
was by such immigrants that the foundation of Baptist principles
was laid in that part of our country. Even now, in conversation
with Norfolk people, we find evidence of their Continental extrac-
tion, for their "speech agreeth thereto," and the Baptist denomination is strongest there in the antique order.

Evans, in his "Early English Baptists" (vol. i., p. 43), gives
the following account of the martyrdom of an English barrister
of the Middle Temple, and styled a knight by Crosby :—

3.—JAMES BAINHAM (SIR)

married the widow of Simon Fish, the author of "The Beggar's
Petition," and this "connexion had excited the suspicions of the

sleepless guardians of the faith. That he was connected with the
Christian brethren appears probable ; and Fox assures us that he
repudiated the baptism of infants."

[It seems only right to interpose the remark here, that certain
words of Bainham quoted by Foxe go so far as to show that he
held also positive views on the question of baptism, for those
words clearly indicate that Bainham regarded as baptism such a
rite only as symbolizes death, burial, and resurrection with Christ.]

" To be suspected, however, was enough. He was called before
the ecclesiastical tribunal. Dissent from the leading doctrines of
the Church was the crime of which he was guilty. Refusing to
recant, he was, with his wife, committed to prison. Sir Thomas
More, who had succeeded Wolsey in the Chancery, was more
learned and had more culture than the great high priest, but he
had more cruelty. By his orders the prisoner was stretched on
the rack and tortured with severity. On the 17th February,
1532, he was carried before the Lord Bishop of London. Suffering from his torture, his spirit failed him, and he abjured his
errors. Fearful as the rack may be, it is feeble as compared with
the pangs of conscious guilt. His misery was unutterable. The
following Sunday the congregation, which had assembled in the
church of St. Augustine, was startled during the service. A man
rose in their midst, pale from recent suffering, holding in his hand
a copy of the New Testament, and with tears flowing down his
cheeks, confessed his crime in denying God in a moment of weakness. ' If,' said he, ' I should not return to the truth, this Word
of God would damn me body and soul at the day of judgment.'
He urged the people to fidelity, declaring that he would not feel
such a hell again for all the world's good.

" The die was now cast. On endless ruin he was now bent.
Spiritually dead, it was the loftiest exercise of mercy on the part
of the spirituality to save him. What mattered a moment's torture
of the body, even the wasting of it at the stake, if the soul could
be saved from everlasting burning ? This doctrine soothed the

conscience, whilst it inflamed the zeal, of the spiritual man. We now find Bainham manacled and in the stocks, in the coal-cellar at Fulham, the residence of his lordship of London. The chill winds of March, and the damp and gloom of his prison, only augmented his zeal. The bishop failing, the chancellor would try his hand. Before him many a criminal had quailed. Will Bainham tremble? Of the power of More's persuasive eloquence we have no record. Of other arguments, the martyrologists give us some report. In his house at Chelsea the confessor was kept, and for two nights was fastened to a post and whipped. The lash drew blood, but it produced no conviction. A week at Fulham was again tried; then the Tower for a fortnight, where the gaoler attempted, but ineffectually, to flog the heresy from him. A month later, sentence was pronounced. The charity of the Church was exhausted, and on April 30, 1532, Smithfield witnessed the blazing faggots which consumed the hero, and the crowd listened to his last words. Thus died one of the noble army of martyrs."

Ivimey, in his "History of the English Baptists," says:— "During the reign of the sanguinary Mary, it is not to be doubted that the Baptists came in for their full share of suffering, and that many of the martyrs were of that denomination, which was then numerous, although their sentiments have not been handed down to us upon that subject."

We have an account of the examination of

4.—RICHARD WOODMAN

—a worker in iron—of Warbleton, in Sussex—before the Bishop of Winchester, in the church of St. Mary Overy's, during the first year of Mary's reign (1553.) In the course of the enquiry, the bishop said "Hold him a book: if he refuse to swear he is an Anabaptist, and shall be excommunicated." Woodman was burned in company with nine others who, it is observed, "were all at large, some say, the very day before they were committed to the flames. No time was allowed for a writ to come down from

E

London to Lewes, in the county of Sussex, where they suffered.
Such legal proceedings were then scarcely thought of. The process of the murderers was like that of the Babylonian tyrant on
the plains of Dura. Whosoever would not worship the idols, was
seized, bound, and cast into the fire."

The following concerning

5.—EDWARD WIGHTMAN

is also given by Ivimey:—James I. "in order to show his zeal against
heresy, took an opportunity to exercise it, by burning alive two of
his subjects. These were Bartholomew Legate, who was charged
with Arianism, and burnt in Smithfield, March 18, 1611;—and
Edward Wightman, a Baptist, of the town of Burton-upon-Trent,
who was convicted December 14, 1611, of divers heresies, before the
Bishop of Lichfield and Coventry; and, being delivered up to the
secular power, was burnt at Lichfield on the 11th April following.

"Amongst other charges brought against him are these:—
'That the baptizing of infants is an abominable custom, that the
Lord's Supper and baptism are not to be celebrated as they are
now practised in the Church of England; and that Christianity
is not wholly professed and preached in the Church of England,
but only in part.'

"Who would have thought that a person would have been burnt
by Protestants for holding such opinions! Happily for our native
country, this day of bigotry is passed, and Edward Wightman
was the last who suffered death in this way. It is rather a curious
fact, that on the supposition of William Sawtry, the Lollard,
opposing infant baptism, which is highly probable, the Baptists
have had the honour of leading the van, and bringing up the rear
of that part of the noble army of English martyrs, who have laid
down their lives at the stake."

Now begin examples of Baptist martyrs who suffered in the
effort to gain general religious freedom, rather than in the defence
of their own distinctive principles.

Anne Askew and Joan Boucher were associated "in the good work of circulating books and tracts in the court of Henry VIII. The probability—says J. Newton Brown, of Philadelphia, in his *Baptist Martyrs*—that these two friends entertained the same views on the subject of baptism, seems confirmed by uncontradicted tradition, and the fact that no other body of Christians ever seems to have claimed either the one or the other."

G.—ANNE ASKEW

" was the intimate friend and companion of the lovely Queen Catherine Parr, and was singled out by the crafty Bishop Gardiner and others, as well as by the popish ladies of the court, hoping that through her they might find an accusation against the queen, for holding the faith and principles of the Reformation."

C. B. Tayler (a clergyman of the Church of England), in his "Memorials of the English Martyrs," says, "Perhaps the most interesting victim of the fires of Smithfield was the celebrated Anne Askew." She had been obliged by her father to marry the widower of her deceased sister—a harsh and bigoted papist. "Being compelled to come up to London (from Kelsey in Lincolnshire), to sue for a divorce, the persecution of her husband and the popish priests followed her, and she fell into the toils which they had laid for her." Remarkable shrewdness, not devoid of a simple humor, was manifest in her replies at the various examinations she had to undergo. But, because she would not divulge who were Protestants at court, the Lord Chancellor and Rich took pains to rack her with their own hands till she was nigh dead.

" Unable to walk or stand from the tortures she had suffered," says Tayler, "poor Anne Askew was carried in a chair to Smithfield, and when brought to the stake, was fastened to it by a chain which held up her body, and one who beheld her there, describes her as ' having an angel's countenance, and a smiling face.' At the very last, a written pardon from the King was offered to her, upon condition that she would recant. The fearless lady turned away her eyes and would not look upon it. She told them that she came not thither to deny her Lord and Master. The fire was ordered to be put under her, 'and thus,' to use the words of John Foxe, 'the good Anne Askew . . . . having passed through so many torments, having now ended the long course of her agonies, being compassed in with flames of fire as a blessed sacrifice unto God, she slept in the Lord, A.D. 1546, (July 16th), leaving behind her a singular example of Christian constancy for all men to follow.'"

7.—JOAN BOUCHER

—more frequently called *Joan of Kent*—says J. Newton Brown— "was unquestionably a Baptist. Uninterrupted and uncontradicted tradition reports her as a member of the Baptist Church, then meeting at Canterbury and Eythorne, and which still flourishes in the latter place, near the south-eastern extremity of England, a few miles from Dover, and about sixteen miles from Canterbury, where not a few of her friends endured the fire of martyrdom.

"Strange as it may appear to some of our readers, in 1547 was established a Protestant inquisition, of which Cranmer and Latimer, who were themselves in after years martyrs, and other men of great eminence, were commissioners. Only eighteen days after the commission was issued, Joan Boucher was arraigned for heresy before this body, and her sentence formally pronounced."

Burnet, in his "History of the Reformation," (Vol. II. p. 112), says :—"When the compassionate young king could not be prevailed upon to sign the warrant for her execution, Cranmer, with his superior learning, was employed to persuade him. He argued from the practice of the Jewish Church in stoning blasphemers, which rather silenced his highness than satisfied him : for when, at last, he yielded to the importunity of the archbishop, he told him with tears in his eyes, that if he did wrong, since it was in submission to his authority, he should answer it before God. This struck the archbishop with surprise, but yet he at last suffered the sentence to be executed." On the 2nd of May, 1550, Joan Boucher appeared at the stake in Smithfield, and there, in spite of efforts made to shake her confidence, "she closely adhered to those words of truth which were her joy and strength in the moments of her dying agony. She loved and adored the holy and immaculate Lamb of God," although one of the charges brought against her had been that of gross misbelief concerning His incarnation.

8.—John James,

minister of the seventh-day Baptist Church meeting in Bulstake Alley, Whitechapel, was apprehended whilst preaching, at the close of 1660, upon a charge of having spoken against King Charles II. Members of his congregation were brought up as witnesses against him, but when pretended extracts from his sermon were read over to them, and the question was put "how could they hear such things as those? they unanimously replied in the fear of the Lord, 'That they never heard such words, as they shall answer it before the Lord, and they durst not lie.'" His wife attempted to plead with the King, but at the mention of the name, Charles "held up his finger and said, 'Oh! Mr. James, he is a sweet gentleman'; but, following him for some further answer, the door was shut against her." The next morning she attended again; and an opportunity soon presenting itself, she implored his Majesty's answer to her request, who then replied, 'That he was a rogue, and should be hanged.' Being brought to the bar to receive sentence (there was no real trial for him), he was asked what he had to say for himself why sentence of death should not be passed upon him, and answered in a few words of scripture wonderfully apposite for the occasion, "Which being spoken, they silenced him, and the court proceeded to sentence; and the judge pronounced sentence of death against him," according to which he was hanged, drawn, quartered, &c., at Tyburn, November 26, 1661. His last words were, "Father, into Thy hands I commit my spirit."

Benjamin and William Hewling were grandsons of the venerable William Kiffin, of Baptist notoriety. They were sacrificed in
the struggle for liberty during the reign of the infamous James
II. Noble, the historian, thus speaks of them :—"These two
amiable, but unfortunate gentlemen, were the only sons of Mr.
Benjamin Hewling, a Turkey merchant of great fortune in London, who, happily for himself, died before them. After their
father's death they were most carefully brought up by a tender
mother, and their maternal grandfather, Mr. William Kiffin, who
though very much advanced in years, as well as his wife, survived them both." From Kiffin's account we gather that—

9.—BENJAMIN HEWLING

joined himself to the Duke of Monmouth against the King, but
they were defeated in the first fight. Benjamin and his brother
William then attempted flight by sea, but they were driven back,
(presumably by adverse weather), were taken prisoners, and
brought to Newgate. Their trial, of course, resulted in sentence
of death, 'as their own words were, for the English liberties, and
the Protestant religion.'

10.—WILLIAM HEWLING

was executed at Lyme, September 12, 1685, at the early age of
nineteen years ; and Benjamin at Taunton, eighteen days later,
aged twenty-two years.

Brave young men ! true Baptists indeed, but proving by their
patriotism that they were Englishmen first and Baptists afterwards. Or, shall we not rather say, they were Christians right
through, and thoroughly Christian, hence their loyalty both to
conscience and to country ? "When just departing out of the
world, with a joyful countenance William Hewling said, 'Oh,
now my joy and comfort is that I have a Christ to go to' ; and so
sweetly resinged his spirit to Christ." When Benjamin was ready
to be offered, " he requested, that he and his fellow-martyrs might

sing a hymn. The sheriff told him it must be with the rope about
their necks ; which they cheerfully accepted, and sung with such
heavenly joy and sweetness, that many who were present said, that
it both broke and rejoiced their hearts. Thus, in the experience
of the delightfulness of praising God on earth, he willingly closed
his eyes on a vain world to pass to that eternal enjoyment . . A
great officer in the King's army was often heard to say, 'If you
would learn to die, go to the young men of Taunton.' "

11.—" ELIZABETH GAUNT (MRS.)

—a Baptist in humble life, was charged with harboring a man
and his family, named Burton, who was suspected of being concerned in the Rye-house plot." The following is Bishop Burnet's
statement of the whole affair:—" There was in London one
Gaunt, a woman that was an Anabaptist, who spent a great part
of her life in arts of charity, visiting the jails, and looking after the
poor, of what persuasion soever they were. One of the rebels
found her out, and she harbored him in her house, and
was looking for an occasion of sending him out of the
kingdom. He went about in the night, and came to hear
what the King had said, viz., that he would sooner pardon
the rebels than those who harbored them. So he, by an
unheard-of baseness, went and delivered himself up, and accused
her that had harbored him. She was seized on and tried. There
was no witness to prove that she knew the person she harbored
was a rebel, except he himself. Her maid witnessed only that he
was entertained at her house ; but though her crime was that of
harboring a traitor, and was proved only by this infamous witness,
yet the judge charged the jury to bring her in guilty, pretending
that the maid was a second witness, though she knew nothing of
that which was the criminal part."

She was condemned and burnt, as the law directs in the case
of women convicted of treason. She died with a constancy even
to cheerfulness, that struck all who saw it. She said, Charity

was a part of her religion as well as faith ; this at worst was feeding an enemy. So she hoped she had reward with Him for whose sake she did this service, how unworthy soever the person was who made so ill a return for it. She rejoiced that God had honored her to be the first that suffered by fire in this reign, and that her suffering was a martyrdom for that religion which was all love. Penn, the Quaker, told me that he saw her die. She laid the straw about her speedily, and behaved herself in such a manner that all the spectators melted in tears." She was executed according to her sentence, at Tyburn, near London, October 23, 1685.

"Richard Baxter somewhere says, that he ' could as soon die for Charity as for any article of the Creed.' While he was *uttering* this just and beautiful sentiment, Elizabeth Gaunt was *exemplifying it in the flames."* (J. Newton Brown.)

Last of all, and coming to *modern times,* we have the name of a

III.—*Baptist Martyr in one of our Colonies.*—As a witness for political justice,

GEORGE WILLIAM GORDON

may fairly be mentioned in the list of those Baptists who have died for their convictions. We have not forgotten the outbreak in Jamaica fifteen years ago. For a long time previously the island had been in an unquiet state, and its troubles were really "a survival of the slave system." The disturbances of 1865, however, had a more direct cause. Certain lands had been allowed to run out of cultivation, and the Crown officials had given the negroes permission to cultivate them, on the condition that they should pay the arrears of quit-rent then due. This was naturally resented by the owners of estate, and no sooner did the negroes begin to avail themselves of the privilege, than an agent of one of the estates attempted to evict one of them from his holding. This led to legal proceedings, which were still pending when the insurrection broke out.

Mr. Justin McCarthy, M.P., in his "History of our own Times,"
(Vol. IV., p. 33 sq.) has given so admirable a review of this case
that we cannot do better than take his account, leaving the reader
to judge whether Gordon is, or is not, fitly classed as a martyr—

"On October 7, 1865, some disturbances took place on the
occasion of a magisterial meeting at Morant Bay, a small town on
the south-east corner of the island. The negroes appeared to be
in an excited state, and many persons believed that an outbreak
was at hand. An application was made to the Governor for
military assistance. The Governor of Jamaica was Mr. Edwaad
John Eyre, who had been a successful explorer in Central, West,
and Southern Australia, had acted as resident magistrate and
protector of aborigines in the region of the Lower Murray in
Australia, and had afterwards been Lieutenant-Governor of New
Zealand, of the Leeward Islands, and of other places. All Mr.
Eyre's dealings with native races up to this time would seem to
have earned for him the reputation of a just and humane
man . . . .

"On October 13, the Governor proclaimed the whole of the
county of Surrey, with the exception of the city of Kingston, under
martial law . . . . At this time, Jamaica was ruled by the
Governor and Council, and the House of Assembly . . . .
Among the members of the Assembly was a coloured man of some
education and property, George William Gordon. Gordon was a
Baptist by religion, and had in him a good deal of the fanatical
earnestness of the field-preacher. He was a vehement agitator
and a devoted advocate of what he considered to be the rights of
the negroes. He appears to have had a certain amount of eloquence,
partly of the conventicle and partly of the stump. He was just
the sort of man to make himself a nuisance to white colonists and
officials who wanted to have everything their own way. Indeed,
he belonged to that order of men who are almost sure to be
always found in opposition to officialism of any kind. Such a
man may do mischief sometimes, but it is certain that out of his

very restlessness and troublesomeness he often does good. No really sensible politician would like to see a Legislative Assembly of any kind without some men of the type of Gordon representing the check of perpetual opposition . . . . He had been appointed churchwarden, was declared disqualified for the office in consequence of his having become a 'Native Baptist,' and he had brought an action to recover what he held to be his rights. He had come to hold the position of champion of the rights and claims of the black man against the white. He was a sort of constitutional opposition in himself. The Governor seems to have at once adopted the conclusion urged on him by others, that Gordon was at the bottom of the insurrectionary movement . . . . There does not seem to have been one particle of evidence to connect Gordon with a rebellious movement more than there would have been to condemn Mr. Bright as a promoter of rebellion, if the working men of the Reform period . . . . had been drawn into some fatal conflict with the police . . . . We have mentioned the fact, that in proclaiming the county of Surrey under martial law, Mr. Eyre had specially excepted the city of Kingston. Mr. Gordon lived near Kingston, and had a place of business in the city ; and he seems to have been there attending to his business, as usual, during the days while the disturbances were going on. The Governor ordered a warrant to be issued for Gordon's arrest. When this fact became known to Gordon, he went to the house of the General in command of the Forces at Kingston and gave himself up. The Governor had him put at once on board a war steamer and conveyed to Morant Bay. Having given himself up in a place where martial law did not exist, where the ordinary courts were open, and where, therefore, he would have been tried with all the forms and safeguards of the civil law, he was purposely carried away to a place which had been put under martial law. Here an extraordinary sort of court-martial was sitting. It was composed of two young navy lieutenants and an ensign in one of Her Majesty's West India regiments. Gordon was hurried before this grotesque tribunal, charged with high treason, found guilty, and sentenced to death. The sentence was approved by the officer in command of the troops sent to Morant Bay. It was then submitted to the Governor, and approved by him also. It was carried into effect without much delay. The day following Gordon's conviction was Sunday, and it was not thought seemly to hang a man on the Sabbath. He was allowed, therefore, to live over that day. On the morning of Monday, October 23, Gordon was hanged. He bore his fate with great heroism, and wrote just before his death a letter to his wife, which is full of pathos in its simple and dignified manliness. He died protesting his innocence of any share in disloyal conspiracy or insurrectionary purpose.

"The whole of the proceedings connected with the trial of Gordon were absolutely illegal ; they were illegal from first to last. It is almost impossible to conceive of any transaction more entirely unlawful. Every step in it was a separate outrage on law. But for its tragic end the whole affair would seem to belong to the domain of burlesque rather than to that of sober history."

We Baptists have no need to be ashamed of our ancestry. On the contrary, considering only the great number and the high character of those who were martyrs for the truth of our principles, we have every reason to be proud of it. "Cardinal Hosius, one of the Pope's presidents at the Council of Trent, says, 'if the truth of religion were to be judged of by the readiness and cheerfulness which a man of any sect shows in suffering, then the opinions and persuasions of no sect can be surer than of the Baptists ; since there have been none for these twelve hundred years past that have been more grievously punished, or that have more cheerfully undergone, and even offered themselves to, the most cruel sorts of punishments, than these people.'" "'Anabaptists,' says old

Bishop Latimer, 'were burned in different parts of the kingdom, and went to the stake with good integrity.'"

Be it noted also, that Baptists have nowhere and at no time retaliated upon their enemies, when the balance of power has shifted in their favor.   In this they have been like their Master, "Who when He was reviled, reviled not again, when He suffered, He threatened not." They have been, and still are, consistent supporters of the principle of perfect liberty of conscience and thorough religious equality.

Above all, let it be remembered, that it is for us to keep alive the martyr spirit in these days, though we do not anticipate the martyr's death.   But, to be wholly devoted to God and God's work—to present ourselves a living sacrifice thereunto—is not this reasonable service, and as important in itself, as if we were required to confirm it with our blood ?   If we yield such an offering, Martin Luther's prophecy will be fulfilled in us :—

> "Flung to the heedless winds,
>   Or on the waters cast,
> Their ashes shall be watched,
>   And gathered at the last :
> And from that scattered dust,
>   Around us and abroad,
> Shall spring a plenteous seed
>   Of witnesses for God.
> Jesus hath now received
>   Their latest dying breath ;
> Yet vain is Satan's boast
>   Of victory in their death.
> Still, still, though dead, they speak,
>   And, triumph-tongued, proclaim
> To many a wakening land
>   The one availing Name."

" Wherefore seeing we also are compassed about with so great a cloud of witnesses, (μάρτυρες), let us lay aside every weight,

and the sin which doth so easily beset us, and let us run with
patience the race that is set before us, looking unto Jesus the
author and finisher of our faith ; who for the joy that was set
before Him endured the cross, despising the shame, and is set
down at the right hand of the throne of God."

What sound is this I hear ?
'Tis one of joyous song—
Of many voices blending clear
From one triumphant throng.
They once the toil endured,
As we now labor hard,
They e'en to pain become inured,
Hence now their full reward.
Already morning breaks,
Our hearts are beating high,
The night is o'er, and golden streaks
Tell Truth's great day is nigh.

SOME SEVENTEENTH CENTURY BAPTISTS:

DENNE—KEACH—BUNYAN; AND OTHERS,

BY

W. HARVEY SMITH.

JAMES the First was dead, and his son Charles the First reigned in his stead. Charles the First figured before the world as the nominal ruler of the people of England, but he himself was ruled by personal vanity. By this passion he appears to have been as completely enthralled and swayed, as is the drunkard by his cups, or the libertine by his lusts.

As might be expected under the rule of such a King, England was neither prosperous at home nor respected abroad. The law ceased to be respected ; the people were ignorant, debased, and discontented ; and Religion was at a terribly low ebb. " Like Priest, like people," is an old adage, and when the King is the head of the Church, perhaps it ought not to be expected that the national religion of the day should reach a much higher standard han the religion of the King. In James the First's reign, the preaching of the Word was entrusted to sorely incapable men, as is seen in a letter written by *Archbishop Abbot* in 1622, three years before the death of James. In this letter addressed to the Clergy, he says :—" His Majesty is much grieved at the heart, to hear of, every day, so much defection from our religion, both to *Popery* and *Anabaptism,* or other points of separation in other parts of the

Kingdom ; and he attributes these defections, in great measure, to the *lightness, affectedness,* and *unprofitableness* of that kind of preaching which hath become of late too much taken up with in our Universities, Cities, and Towns." After a little fuller description, he adds :—" Now the people bred up with this kind of teaching, and never instructed in the Catechism and fundamental grounds of religion, are for all this *airy nourishment,* no better than *'New table books,'* ready to be filled up with the manuals or Catechisms of Popish Priests, or the papers and pamphlets of Anabaptists, Brownists, and Puritans." This does not say much for the religious teaching of that day, even in the principal seats of learning ; and we may safely conclude that the bulk of the country was in a far worse state.

In Charles the First's reign, the Clergy of the rural districts were " mere readers of prayers ;" and on this account they were styled " *Reading Vicars,*" " *Reading Curates,*" &c. But what is far worse, in addition to their incapacity for preaching, " they were for the most part immoral and dissolute ;" and the religion of the " Book of Sports" was in full swing. In 1618, James issued a declaration to the effect, " that on Sun lays, after Divine service, no lawful recreation should be barred from his good people, which should not tend to a breach of the laws of his Kingdom, or the canons of his Church. The sports specified were dancing, archery, leaping, vaulting, May-games, Whitsunales, Morrice-dances, and the setting up of May-poles."

This declaration was ordered to be read in the parish Churches ; Nonconformists and all who refused to attend Church, being prohibited from taking part in the sports. Charles had republished the said declaration, with an order that it be read in all the Churches of the land ; severe penalties being imposed on any Clergyman who refused compliance with the order. Is it singular that with such a law the masses of the people were steeped in irreligion and vice, and that persecution of honest and good men had free course ?

In a petition presented by a persecuted Baptist about this period, the writer says :—" Our miseries are long, and lingering imprisonments for many years, in divers counties of England, in which many have died and left behind them widows and many small children ; taking away our goods, and others the like of which we can make probation ; not for any disloyalty to your Majesty, nor hurt to any mortal man—our adversaries themselves being judges—but only because we dare not assent unto, and practice in the Worship of God, such things as we have not faith in, because it is sin against the Most High."

During the reign of Martial Law, and under the rule of the bold " *Protector,*" the Baptists, with other Dissenters, enjoyed a season of rest, and, like the Apostolic Churches, " grew and multiplied." But though not actively persecuted, they were much despised : every man's tongue was against them. Papists, Episcopalians, Presbyterians, Independents, all alike heaped reproach upon them.

The noble Cromwell passed away, the Stuarts were restored, and Charles the Second ascended the English throne. In direct violation of his solemn promise to allow freedom of conscience in matters religious, this false son of a false father commenced at once the persecution of all Dissenters. An old act of Elizabeth was revived, which decreed that all who refused to attend Church should be fined £20 per month ; and under this act great numbers were siezed and cast into prison until the money should be forthcoming. " It is estimated that during this reign, upwards of 8,000 dissenters died in prison," amongst whom were a large number of Baptists. This state of things continued until the " Declaration of Indulgence " in the year 1672.

That the Baptists were a somewhat numerous body at the beginning of these evil days is certain. Undeniable authority reports at least seven congregations in London, and many more in the provinces, and memorable names figure in their history. One of their preachers, THOMAS LAMB, was arraigned before the revived Star Chamber and sent to gaol. THOMAS BREWER was imprisoned for fourteen years. SAMUEL HOWE, "a popular Baptist preacher, during this reign died in prison, and was buried like a dog in the highway." He wrote and published a book, entitled, "The Sufficiency of the Spirit's Teaching, without Human Learning," on the title page of which appeared the following lines :—

"What *How?* how now ? hath How such learning found,
To throw art's curious image to the ground ?
Cambridge and Oxford may their glory now,
Veil to a Cobbler, if they know but *How ?*"

Roger Williams says of him : " Amongst so many instances, dead and living, to the everlasting praise of Jesus Christ, and of His Holy Spirit, breathing and blessing where He listeth, I cannot but with honourable testimony remember that eminent Christian witness and prophet of Christ, even that despised and yet beloved *Samuel Howe*, who being by calling a cobbler, and without learning (which yet in its sphere and place he honoured), who yet, I say, by searching the Holy Scriptures, grew so excellent a textuary, or Scripture-learned man, that few of those Rabbis, who scorned to mend or make a shoe, could aptly or readily, from the Holy Scriptures, outgo him." His life and death were honourable, and though buried in the highway, and in spite of the troublous state of the times, his funeral was attended by hundreds of godly men.

HENRY DENNE,

a noted Baptist of this time, was educated at the University of Cambridge, ordained by the Bishop of St. David's, in or about the year 1630, and appointed to the "living" of Pyrton, in Hertfordshire. This living he held for ten years, and acquired a well-deserved celebrity as a faithful pastor and instructive preacher. His fearlessness as a preacher may be seen in the following fact. Appointed to preach the "Visitation Sermon" at

F

Baldock, in 1641, he took for his text, John v. 35. In the course of his sermon he boldly denounced the pride and covetousness of the clergy—their pluralities—their neglect of duty by non-residence, and other evils ; and like the prophet to whom his text referred, he sternly demanded reformation. " I must call upon those in authority," he said, " to make diligent search after these foxes. If the courts had been as vigilant to find out these as in hunting out Non-conformists, surely by this time the Church would have been as free from them as the land is from wolves; but they have preferred the traditions of men before the commandments of Almighty God. I tell you that Conformity hath ever sped the worse for their sakes, who, breaking the commandments of God, think to make amends by conforming to the traditions of men."

After such a declaration, we do not much marvel to find him ere long turning his back upon a corrupt Church and casting in his lot with the despised Dissenters. In the early part of 1643, he was baptised by Thomas Lamb, then pastor of the Baptist Church meeting in Bell Alley, Coleman Street, London. Henry Denne now became a "General Baptist" HOME MISSIONARY, preaching the Gospel with great success throughout the counties of Staffordshire and Cambridgeshire, and establishing many new churches. Like his Lord and Master he soon made enemies. He was arrested and imprisoned at Cambridge, but through the intervention of friends, was removed thence to the "Peterhouse Prison," Aldersgate Street, London.

Mr. Denne was soon released, and such was the confused state of the times, that he (though a pronounced Baptist) was appointed minister of Eltisley Parish Church, in Cambridgeshire ; from which place he travelled as before, in all directions, preaching and baptizing. In 1645, in the course of his mission tour, he visited the County of Kent, and many through his labours were added to the despised sect in that region. Soon after we find him in the Parliamentary army—but as a soldier he still continued his evangelistic work, and while " Cornet Denne" was his military title

—"Parson Denne" was the name by which he was best known among his comrades.

While in the army he narrowly escaped death as a mutineer. In May, 1649, he took part in a mutiny of his regiment, partly occasioned by unwillingness to join the expedition to Ireland, and partly by a general discontent with the conduct of affairs. The mutiny was promptly quelled, and Cornet Denne, with three others, was sentenced to be shot.

Denne was a man of sterling piety and sound common sense; and realising at once the folly of his action, and the terrible consequences which might have resulted from his success, he acknowledged the justness of his sentence. He said, that although his heart could not accuse him of an evil meaning, yet he was convinced of the evil of his action, and that if they had continued three or four days longer, the land would have been plunged in misery and ruin.

The other three were shot, and Denne was led to the place of execution, expecting a like fate, but on arriving at this spot, Lieutenant-General Cromwell informed him that the General in command had extended mercy to him. Whereupon he exclaimed, "I am not worthy of such a mercy; I am more ashamed to live, than afraid to die."

Next we find him at a meeting of the Baptist Church at Fenstanton, exhorting the brethren to *home missionary* labours. As the result of this address, he with another, was sent out on a missionary excursion, an account of which was given on their return. The year following, he was invited to the pastorate of the Baptist Church at Canterbury. The Fenstanton Church—recognizing the greater need of her sister Church—gladly consented, and furnished a companion, money, and horses for the journey.

A Clergyman of the Church of England is accredited with writing the following epitaph for his tomb—

"To tell his wisdom, learning, goodness unto men,
    I need to say no more, but—here lies Henry Denne."

FRANCIS CORNWELL, M.A.

was educated at Emanuel College, Cambridge, and afterwards became Vicar of Marden, in Kent. For refusal to conform to certain ceremonies, imposed by Archbishop Laud, he was committed to Maidstone Jail. While there, one of his parishoners, being much exercised in her mind, sought his advice on the subject of Baptism. He marshalled up his most powerful arguments, but in vain. His failure led him to further research, he became convinced of the unscripturalness of " Infant Baptism ;" and, true to his conviction, was baptized by Mr. William Jeffery, an eminent Baptist Minister.

Appointed soon after to preach before an assembly of Divines at Cranbrook, he chose for his text, Mark viii. 7. " Howbeit in vain do they worship me, teaching for doctrines the commandments of men." He told his hearers that " *Infant Baptism* was an antichristian innovation, a human tradition, and a practice for which there was neither precept nor true deduction from the Word of God." As might be expected, an animated discussion followed this unpalatable discourse, in which passion was made to play the part of logic. One Clergyman who was present took down the sermon in shorthand, and undertook to prepare a reply, but the only reply he could give was to submit himself to the ordinance of " Believers' Baptism," which he did in the course of a few months.

Mr. Cornwell published a work on Baptism, entitled, " A vindication of the Royal Commission of King Jesus." This book was freely circulated amongst the Members of the House of Commons, and produced great excitement. He formed a Baptist Church in the neighbourhood of Cranbrook, over which he presided till his death. Neal says, " He was one of the most learned divines that espoused the Baptist cause."

CHRISTOPHER BLACKWOOD,

the Clergyman who was converted to Baptist principles by his attempt to refute the arguments of the last named, was born in

1606, graduated at Cambridge in 1624, and became Curate of Rye, in Sussex. On his secession to the Baptists, he was elected to the Pastorate of a Church at Spillshill, near Staplehurst, Kent. He afterwards served in Cromwell's army. Then we find him pastor of a Church in Dublin, and taking a general oversight of the Baptists in Ireland. He was a learned man, and a jealous advocate for religious liberty. One of his books on this subject was entitled, "The storming of antichrist in his two last and strongest garrisons—*Compulsion of Conscience*, and *Infant Baptism*."

Benjamin Keach,

another famous Baptist, was one of the earliest Pastors of the Church, now meeting in the "Metropolitan Tabernacle," and over which the Rev. C. H. Spurgeon has long and ably presided, a most worthy successor of worthy men.

Mr. Keach wrote a small book entitled, "The Child's Instructor; or, a New and Easy Primer," inculcating Baptist principles amongst others. He also affirms, that "Christ's true ministers have not their learning and wisdom from men, nor from Universities, nor from human schools—for human learning, arts, and sciences, are not essential to the making of a good minister—but only the gift of God, which cannot be bought with silver or gold." "Also, they are not lords over God's heritage—they rule them not by force and cruelty, neither have they power to force and compel men to believe and obey their doctrines, but are only to persuade and entreat ; this is the way of the Gospel as Christ taught them."

For publishing this book he was arrested, and indicted at the assizes as follows :—

"Thou art here indicted, by the name of Benjamin Keach, of Winslow, in the county of Buckinghamshire, for that thou, being a *seditious, heretical,* and *schismatical* person, evilly and *maliciously* disposed and disaffected to his Majesty's government of the Church of England, didst maliciously and wickedly, on the first day of May, in the seventeenth year of our Sovereign Lord

the King, write, print, and publish, or cause to be written, printed, and published, one seditious and venemous book, entitled, 'The Child's Instructor,' wherein are contained, by way of question and answer, these damnable positions, contrary to the Book of Common Prayer and the Liturgy of the Church of England." Of this heinous crime he was duly convicted, and sentenced as follows :—
"Benjamin Keach, you are here convicted for writing, printing, and publishing a seditious and schismatical book, for which the Court's judgment is this, and the Court doth award—that you shall go to jail for a fortnight, with out bail or mainprize, and the next Saturday to stand upon the pillory at Aylesbury in the open Market, for the space of two hours—from eleven of the clock till one—with a paper upon your head with this inscription : 'For writing, printing, and publishing a schismatical book entitled, "The Child's Instructor." ' And the next Thursday to stand in the same manner and for the same time in the market of Winslow ; and there your book shall be openly burnt before your face by the common hangman, in disgrace of you and your doctrine. And you shall forfeit to the King's Majesty the sum of £20, and shall remain in prison until you find sureties for your good behaviour and appearance at the assizes—there to renounce your doctrines and to make such public submission as shall be enjoined you."

The sentence was fully carried out ; and at eleven o'clock on the Saturday morning—as if he were a wretch, convicted of some infamous offence—this faithful servant of God was placed in the pillory at Aylesbury. Imagine a man set in an upright wooden frame with three holes, his head through one and his hands through the other two : a paper on his head stating his crime ; and the whole fixed on a raised platform, in the centre of a Market-place on a Market-day, with a gaping multitude of country people all around—some sympathising and others jeering, and you have at once a rough picture of the scene.

On his way to the Market-place, he cheerfully remarked to his sorrowing friends who accompanied him, "The *Cross is the way to the*

Crown." When his head and hands were fixed in the pillory, he addressed the crowd as follows :—" Good people, I am not ashamed to stand here this day, with this paper on my head ; my Lord Jesus was not ashamed to suffer on the Cross for me, and it is for His cause I am made a gazing stock. Take notice, it is not for any wickedness that I stand here, but for writing and publishing His truths, which the Spirit of the Lord hath revealed in the Holy Scriptures."

A Clergyman called out : " No, Mr. Keach, you are there for writing and publishing errors ; and you may now see what your errors have brought you to." This specimen of the bulwark of Christianity, was now himself attacked by the justice-loving farmers about him. One told him of his being pulled drunk out of a ditch : another reminded him he had lately been discovered drunk under a haycock. At this the crowd united in a hearty English display of ridicule ; and this drunken defender of the faith hurried away, let us hope, to repent before the Lord whose cause he had dishonoured, and whose servant he had sought to injure. The following week Keach was subjected to the same indignity at Winslow, where his book was publicly burnt, according to the sentence.

But standing head and shoulders above the Baptists of his time, was

JOHN BUNYAN,

born at Elstow, near to Bedford, in the year 1628. Of his parents we know little excepting that his father was a tinker or brazier, and that they were poor but honest folk. No costly portraits of a lordly ancestry lined the walls of their humble village home, nor were any traditions of former greatness handed down as heirlooms from sire to son. Our hero himself says, " My generation was low and inconsiderable, and my father's house of that rank which is meanest and most despised of all the families of the land."

John—at what age we do not know—was sent to school, where he assures us he " learned to read and write after the rate of other poor men's children." But this knowledge, he confesses with shame, he soon almost entirely lost.

Endowed by nature with a robust frame, an excitable temperament, a strong will, and a vivid imagination, he was the ring-leader of the boys and youths of the neighbourhood, in all kinds of legitimate sports, and in lying, swearing, mischievous pranks, and practical jokes. In common with other healthy, high-spirited lads, he had his share of narrow escapes. Once he fell into a creek of the sea, again he fell into the river Ouse, on both which occasions he barely escaped drowning. Another perilous adventure shows unmistakably the grit of which he was made. Walking in the fields with some companions, an adder crossed his path ; acting on the spur of the moment, the daring lad struck it on the back, thrust open the creature's mouth with his stick, and plucked out its sting with his fingers—thus placing himself in great peril of his life. One cannot but feel that this incident shadows his own internal conflict with the Tempter, and is strangely prophetic of the Bunyan of later life, who dealt such masterly strokes on "*Apollyon,*" and with such marvellous courage and skill, laboured to pluck out the sting from the mouth of "*that old Serpent, the Devil.*"

His early life was singularly wicked, as his after life was singularly good. To argue as Macaulay, Froude, and others have done, that because he was free from the vices of *drunkenness* and *unchastity*, therefore his own bitter condemnations of himself are not to be taken in a literal sense, is, we think, simply to beg the whole question. The most elementary knowledge of human nature would lead us to expect—and Bunyan's plain, unvarnished statement compels us to believe—that his early life was extremely wicked and godless. Whatever Bunyan did, he did *thoroughly.* His nature was such that he could not do anything—not even sin by halves : with him it was the *whole* or *none.* As he was a ring-leader in all kinds of sports, so he assures us that in lying, cursing, swearing, and blaspheming the Holy Name of God, he had few equals. That statement tallies exactly with what we should expect

from such a temperament, with such godless surroundings and
without any Christian training; and any attempt to explain it
away appears to us as the futile hair-splitting of maudlin
sentiment.

In that age, when tyranny and hatred usurped the throne of
Jesus' religion of love; when the baneful superstitions of Rome
imbued the minds of the multitude; when the majority of
preachers voted every one to eternal burnings who could not
pronounce their shibboleths; when ignorant parents threatened
their children with the evil one every time they crossed their
erratic wills; when the most eloquent discourses of brawling
women and effeminate priests, consisted of the horrors of *fire* and
brimstone—it is not very remarkable that young Bunyan's earliest
religious impressions mere made up chiefly of terrible fears and
horrible thoughts of Hell.

His childish dreams were of devils and wicked spirits, who
laboured to drag him down to the pit. While awake, his childish
fancy was occupied with thoughts of dwelling with devils "in
darkness, fire, and chains." Even at the early age of nine or ten
years, when in the midst of his companions, and engaged in little
boyish games, his mind would often revert to these awful things.
So much was this the case that he says, "I often wished that there
were no hell, or that I had been a devil; that if it must needs be
that I must go to hell, I might be rather a tormentor of others
than be tormented myself."

These unnatural and unhealthy religious thought-seeds blown
into his heart by the breath of the all-pervading superstition of
the age, and fostered by injudicious friends, produced, as could
only be expected, unwholesome fruit. His childish thoughts and
dreams, worthy only of a heathen mythology, were succeeded by
an utter callousness to serious subjects. The very thought of
religion was hateful to him; and he would as soon have been in
prison as have listened to anything from a good book. "Then,"
says he, "I said unto God, 'depart from me, for I desire not the

knowledge of thy ways.'" But even in this, the midnight of his soul, one ray of light, like some shooting star, pierces the darkness. The thought of hypocrisy made his heart to quake, and the sound of an oath or a lie from one who professed religion cut him to the quick.

At the age of seventeen we find him in the army, though on which side is a somewhat doubtful point. Macaulay, and indeed most of his biographers, think that he fought on the side of the parliament, and we think they are right, indeed, it is difficult to conceive of Bunyan, as fighting—unless under compulsion—for the cause of such a king as Charles. While in the army on one occasion he was ordered out with a besieging party, but one of the company volunteering to go in his stead, took his place, and while standing sentinel was shot in the head and killed. This marvellous escape failed at the time to produce any effect upon him, and he continued his former wicked course of life.

At twenty he married an orphan girl as poor as himself, the only dowry she brought him being the cherished memory of a godly father, and a parental legacy of two books, entitled, "The Plain Man's Pathway to Heaven," and "The Practice of Piety." Besides, their united wealth in household stuff did not amount to so much as a dish or a spoon. Though such marriages cannot be recommended, yet, in Bunyan's case, it seems to have been a wise step. He read with his wife in the books aforementioned, and frequently conversed with her on the character and habits of her father. Under her almost imperceptible influence, his hatred of religion slowly vanished, like the receding mists before the rising dawn. He was as one awaking out of a heavy, troubled sleep, his mind gradually opening to sacred things, as the mind of the sleeper to the realities of day. At first, he fell into the religious formalism of the time—attended Church twice on the Sunday, and eagerly imbibed the national superstition as to the sacredness of Church and all things pertaining thereto. The building, furniture, vestments, priest, clerk, all received his adoration. So fully did this feeling possess him, that he tells us he would gladly have laid himself down in front of any priest that he might trample upon him—the name, the garb, the work, did so intoxicate and bewitch him. All this time he appears not to have thought of the *guilt* of sin, and Christ as the Saviour of men seems never to have entered his head.

His first thought of sin, as sin, was produced in his mind by a sermon he heard on the wrong of Sabbath-breaking. This unsettled him a little, but in the afternoon of the same day he went to his usual Sunday sports, and entered into them with all his accustomed zest. Whilst engaged in a game of "Cat," he suddenly stopped—a small voice seemed to say to him, "John, wilt thou leave thy sins and go to *Heaven*, or have thy sins and go to *Hell?*" But the pause was only momentary, and the solemn question of the "still small voice" received no answer. A few minutes later there was a break in the game, and looking up, he thought he saw Jesus, who looked on him with hot displeasure. At once the conviction fastened upon him that for him there was no hope—he could not be forgiven. He strove to shake off thoughts of the future, and to take his fill of sin, but in vain, for that look of the "Man of sorrows" was graven deeply on the fleshy tablet of his heart. Very soon after this, at the rebuke of a godless woman, he shook off his habits of swearing and lying. Now began a long conflict, evil thoughts and soul-racking doubt. Now he had sinned the unpardonable sin ; now, like Judas, he had sold his Lord : now he was a reprobate given up to destruction. Sometimes despair gave place to hope. Once he thought he had faith ; now he would put that faith to the test. He went out into the highway, resolved to say to the puddles, "be ye dry," and to the dry places, "be ye puddles ;" but fearing lest the test should fail, and thinking he had better first pray for faith, despair again enveloped his soul. Anon the talk of some devout women at Bedford, who were conversing *joyously* on religion, fired his soul with hope. Conversations with these joyous Christians, and the study of Luther on the *Galatians*, helped him by the way, till at length, after two years of almost unbroken agony, meditation on "Christ Jesus, who of God is made unto us wisdom, and righteousness, and sanctification, and redemption," broke the spell, and peace possessed his soul. The gates of "Doubting Castle" were opened —"Giant Despair" was left far behind—Bunyan had gazed on the Cross—his burden had rolled into the sepulchre—and he went on his way rejoicing.

He was baptised by Mr. Gifford in the river Ouse, at Bedford, and received into fellowship with the Baptist Church there, in the year 1654 ; being then twenty-six years of age.

That he had prospered in worldly matters is evident from the following. When Cromwell dismissed the "Long Parliament," an address was sent from Bedfordshire, approving his conduct, recognising him as the Lord's instrument, and recommending the county magistrates to serve in the Assembly about to be appointed, and among the thirty-six signatures to this address appear the names of Gifford and Bunyan. "This," says Froude, "speaks for itself, he must have been at least a householder and a person of distinction." Another biographer said, "God had increased his stores so that he lived in great credit among his neighbours."

But God had other work for him to do, and another path for him to tread, as will shortly appear. The Baptist friends at Bedford early recognised his gifts, and soon pressed him into work. At first he could only be persuaded to go out with the village preachers and give now and then a short application after others had spoken, but after a while he ventured on more public services. The first time he preached in Bedford the whole town turned out to hear him, so great was the sensation produced by his wonderful change. As they listened to his earnest address, some mocked, but others were deeply impressed.

The state of his mind at this momentous period of his career may be gathered best from his own words : "At first," he says, "I could not believe that God should speak by me to the heart

of any man, still counting myself unworthy : yet those who were
thus touched would love me and have a particular respect for me,
and though I did put it from me that they should be awakened
by me, still they would confess and affirm it before the saints of God.
. . . . "Wherefore, seeing them in both their words and deeds to
be so constant, and also in their hearts so earnestly pressing after the
knowledge of Jesus Christ, rejoicing that God had sent me where
they were, then I began to conclude it might be even so—that
God had owned in His work such a foolish one as I. And
then came that word of God to my heart with such sweet refresh-
ment, 'The blessing of them that were ready to perish, is come
upon me ; yea, I caused the widow's heart to sing for joy.'

"At this, therefore, I rejoiced, yea, the tears of those whom
God had awakened by my preaching, would be both solace and comfort to me. "I thought much on those sayings: 'Who is he then that
maketh me glad, but the same that is made sorry by me ?' And
again : 'If I be not an Apostle unto others, yet doubtless I am to
you ; for the seal of mine apostleship are ye in the Lord.' These
things were as an argument unto me, that God had called me to,
and stood by me, in this work."

His sole thought was now, how best to consecrate his energies
to the service of Christ. He preached all over the Midland
Counties, in London, and other places—in barn or wood, in market-place or quiet alley, in village cottage or town chapel, wherever
there was an open door—and he was soon the most popular
Baptist preacher of his time. This continued for about six years,
when the "*Restoration*," under Charles the Second, gagged his
mouth and stayed his public work. On the evening of November
the 12th, 1660, he was engaged to preach at Samsell, in Bedfordshire. This coming to the magistrates' ears, a warrant was issued
for his apprehension. He was aware of their intention to arrest him,
but following the example of Him who said, "Behold I go up to
Jerusalem," he went to Samsell. His host, at whose house the
meeting was to be held, urged him to flee, but he answered,

"Come, be of good cheer, our cause is good, we need not be ashamed of it; to preach God's Word is so good a work, that we shall be well rewarded hereafter, if we suffer here." He then went out into the fields to meditate. Conflicting thoughts struggled in his mind; he had a family at home—one child was blind—his wife was ill—what should he do? His thoughts on the other side may be surmised as follows : 1. Bold words should be supported by bold action. 2. What will the new converts think, if such an one as I flee? 3. What will the world think if I play the coward? 4. If I am called of God to lead a forlorn hope, it is my duty to set an example to those who shall be my followers in the path of suffering. The conflict was severe, but he triumphed. Taking one lingering heart-look at home, wife, and children, he turned his face to Christ, and in effect said, " My Master expects that every man of His shall do his duty, and by His grace that will I do." The meeting was opened at the time appointed, and when just in the act of commencing his address from the words, " Dost thou believe on the Son of God?" the constables appeared and Bunyan was arrested. He was taken before the magistrates and, after an examination characteristic of the times, committed for trial at the sessions. Substantial bail was offered, but refused on the ground that he would not promise not to preach. Several other attempts were made to bail him out, but in vain. After lying in prison seven weeks, he was brought up at the Quarter Sessions, and indicted before Justice Keeling and others, as follows :—

" That he being a person of such and such a condition, had since such a time, devilishly and perniciously abstained from coming to Church to hear Divine Worship, and was a common upholder of unlawful meetings and conventicles, to the great disturbance and distraction of the good subjects of the kingdom, contrary to the laws of our Sovereign Lord the King."

Bunyan boldly defended himself and sought to prove from the Scriptures his authority and duty to preach the Gospel to his fellow men, but Justice Keeling called his arguments "Pedlar's French," and sternly commanded him to leave off his "canting." And when in his simplicity he asked if it were not his duty to obey God rather than man, another of the judges asked him with a sneer, "Is not your god *Beelzebub*?"

His conviction was a foregone conclusion. He had broken the law of the land, infamous law though it was, and there was no alternative but to convict him. The jury found him guilty, and his sentence was pronounced in this form :— "John Bunyan, you must be had back to prison and there lie for three months following, and if at three months' end you do not submit to go to Church to hear Divine Service and leave off your preaching, you must be banished the realm. And if after such a day as shall be appointed you to be gone, you shall be found in this realm, or be found to come over again without express licence from the King, you must stretch by the neck for it, I tell you plainly." This threat of banishment was never carried out, neither was he again brought before the justices, yet for twelve long years Bunyan remained a prisoner in Bedford Jail.

To such a man, alive all over, his life at blood heat, and his soul all ablaze with "yearning pity for mankind and burning charity," one would have thought this lengthy prison-life beyond the powers of mortal endurance : yet the grace of God sustained him. He was a kind husband and father, and to part from his wife and his poor blind child was, he says, as the "pulling the flesh from his bones." No wonder that he was often and sorely troubled with thoughts of their present and future hardships until almost in despair. But for all this, his prison-life was happier, and a thousandfold more useful for God and man, than even his life at large. His prison walls shut him out from much social intercourse and the society of friends that were dear to him, but they served also to shut him in to more frequent and undisturbed communion with his God and Saviour. Speaking of his prison-life with the object of stirring up the godly to bless God and take courage, he says : "I never had so great an inlet into the Word of God as now. Those Scriptures that I saw nothing in before, were made in this place and state to shine upon me. Jesus Christ was never more real and apparent than now ; here I have seen and felt Him indeed. Oh ! that word, 'We have not preached unto you cunningly devised fables,' and that other, 'God raised Him up from the dead that your faith and hope might be in God,' were blessed words unto me in this imprisoned condition. So that sometimes when I have been in the favour of them I have been able to laugh at destruction, and to fear neither the horse nor his rider. I have had sweet sights of the forgiveness of my sins in this place, and of my being with Jesus in another world. Oh ! the 'Mount Zion,' 'the heavenly Jerusalem,' and the 'spirits of just men made perfect,' and 'God the Judge of all,' and Jesus, have been sweet unto me in this place. I have seen here what I am persuaded I shall never, while in this world, be able to express. I have seen a truth in this scripture, 'Whom having not seen, ye love ; in Whom, though now ye see Him not, yet believing, ye rejoice with joy unspeakable, and full of glory.' I never knew what it was for God to stand by me at all times, and at every offer of Satan to afflict me, as I have found Him since I came in hither. For look how fears have presented themselves, so have supports and encouragements : yea, when I have started, even as it were, at nothing else but my own shadow, yet God has been very tender to me, and hath not suffered me to be molested, but with one scripture or another, strengthened me against all : insomuch that I have often said, 'Were it lawful I would pray for greater trouble, for the greater comfort's sake" . . . . "Many more of the dealings of God towards me I might relate, 'But these out of the spoils won in battle, have I dedicated to maintain the house of God.'"

Like a more ancient prisoner for righteousness' sake, Bunyan seems to have found favour in the eyes of his jailor, and to have enjoyed unusual liberty. He preached to his fellow prisoners ;

he preached occasionally in the woods around : once he journeyed to London ; frequently he spent a day and a night at home, and on several occasions he presided over Church meetings at Bedford. Rumours of the laxity of his imprisonment reached those in authority, and once a messenger was despatched in hot haste to see if these things were so. Bunyan was out and had leave of absence for the night, but a presentiment of something wrong led him to hasten back to the jail, just before midnight. The jailor reprimanded him for not staying out instead of disturbing him at that hour of the night. He had not been in many minutes when the messenger arrived, who demanded to know if the prisoners were all in ward, asked personally after "that fellow Bunyan," and demanded to see him. When he had gone, the jailor said, "Bunyan, you may go out when you like, for you know better when to return than I can tell you."

"In 1672 Charles the Second pardoned about five hundred Quakers, who had been languishing in prison for not attending the services of the Church. Upon this Bunyan and his fellow-prisoners at Bedford petitioned for liberty, and at a Court of Privy Council at Whitehall, held on the 17th of May, 1672, present the King and twenty-four of his councillors, the following minute was made : "Whereas by order of the Board of the 8th instant, the humble petition of John Penn, John Bunyan, John Dunn, Thomas Haynes, Simon Haynes, and George Parr, prisoners in the goale at Bedford, convicted upon several statutes for not conforming to the rights and ceremonies of the Church of England, and for being at unlawful meetings, was referred to the Sheriff of the County of Bedford, who was required to certify this Board whether the said persons were committed for the crimes in the said petition mentioned, *and for no other;* which he having accordingly done by his certificate of the 11th instant, It was thereupon, this day, ordered by his Majesty in Council, that the said petition and certificate be (and herewith) sent to his Majesty's Attorney-General, who is authorised, and required

G

to insert them into the general pardon to be passed for the Quakers.'"

Thus at length, Bunyan was released, his release being speedily followed by the "Act of Indulgence," and from this time he ceased not to preach and to teach with untiring zeal. He was also much in request as a peace-maker, and it was while returning from a journey to Reading, whither he had gone to reconcile a father and son, that he took the severe cold which resulted in his death.

"He died at the house of one Mr. Strudwick, a grocer, at the Star, on Snow Hill, on the 12th of August, 1688, and was buried in the new burying ground, near the Artillery Ground, now known as 'Bunhill Fields,' where his tomb may still be seen."

BUNYAN THE PREACHER

attracted great multitudes. It was no uncommon thing for him to have, when in London, an audience of twelve hundred people at seven o'clock on a cold winter's morning. On one recorded occasion three thousand gathered to hear him in Southwark. His marvellous success was owing to the fact that he preached only the realities of his own experience and convictions.

He preached to the "dead in trespasses and sins," as one raised from the dead; to the awakened, as one who had sought and found; to the tempted, as one who had himself suffered being tempted; and to the sceptical, as one who had himself—with reeling brain, and "swimming, swollen, senselessness of soul"— paced the damp and gloomy cells of "Doubting Castle." To the sorrowing, to the straitened, and to the struggling, his word came as from one who had himself sounded the deep, and fought, as for very life, with the surging waves of adversity. He preached to the sleepy disciples, as one who, having broken the spell of drowsiness, had watched in the garden, had seen the agony, and was wide awake with an all-constraining and self-consuming love. While to the babes in Christ he spake as one who had not forgotten his own childhood, but becoming a man in Christ Jesus, had cast off childish littleness in talk and character.

His preaching was realistic ; the preacher and his word were real ; sin and salvation were real ; God and Christ were real. The Holy Spirit was a real present power, while before him were real men and women in real danger or in real safety, and with real needs of various kinds.

He says :—" Oh ! that they who have heard me speak, did but see as I do, what sin, death, hell, and the curse of God is ; and also what the grace, and love, and mercy of God is through Christ, to men in such a case as they are—who are yet estranged from Him." "And indeed I did often say in my heart before the Lord, ' that if I be hanged up presently before their eyes, it would be a means to awaken them and confirm them in the truth, and I should be contented.' " Again speaking of the realized presence of God in his preaching, especially when speaking on "life by Christ without works," he says, "Oh ! it hath been with such power and heavenly evidence upon my own soul, that I could not be contented with saying, ' I believe and am sure,' methought I was more than sure that those things were true."

Genius alone was not the grand secret of Bunyan's success, but *reality*, which is the soul of genius. His natural genius without his reality would have been as powerless as the most muscular frame without life, and the most ingenious machine without its propelling force. Reality produces reality, and a real man cannot but do real work. No wonder that Dr. Owen, chaplain to the King, when asked by his Majesty how he, a learned man, could go and hear a tinker preach, answered, " If I could have the tinker's power, I would give all my learning to get hold of it."

As a Writer of Allegory,

Bunyan stands alone, unsurpassed and unequalled. The highest skill of the painter is shown in the reality of his painting—in his power to make his human figures speak, his fields " stand dressed in living green," and his flowers almost send forth their varied scent. The success of an allegorist is shown in like manner. Bunyan displayed this power in a very high degree—hence his fame. At first, and indeed for a long time, his power was scarcely recognised save by the lower and middle-classes of society.

But Cowper, Johnson, Scott, Coleridge, Southey, Macaulay, and a host of other learned critics have given him unstinted praise, and Dean Stanley has recommended, that if anyone has read his "Pilgrim's Progress" ninety-nine times, he should at once begin to read it the hundredth.

Macaulay says of this book—"Every reader knows the straight and narrow path, as well as he knows a road in which he has gone backward and forward a hundred times. This is the highest miracle of genius—that things that are not, should be as though they were—that the imaginations of one mind should become the personal recollections of another. And this miracle the tinker wrought. There is no ascent, no declivity, no resting-place, no turnstile with which we are not perfectly acquainted—the tall and swarthy Madam Bubble, Mr. Worldly-Wiseman, and my Lord Hate-Good, Mr. Talkative, and Mrs. Timorous, are all actually existing beings to us."

"Bunyan is almost the only writer who gave to the abstract the interest of the concrete—the spirit of beauty, the principle of good, the principle of evil, when he treated of them, ceased to be abstractions. They took shape and colour: they were no longer mere words, but 'intelligible forms,' 'fair humanities,' objects of love, of adoration, or of fear."

In the judgment of Macaulay, Bunyan is one of the only two men of genius produced by the 17th century.

BUNYAN WAS A BAPTIST.

Some writers have laboured hard to prove that he was not, but every faithful and impartial Biographer has honestly assigned him to us. "Facts are stubborn things;" and the facts in this case are unanswerable.

He was baptized: he was received into fellowship with a Baptist Church. He never left that fellowship for any other. He was chosen pastor of that same Church. He held the office of pastor over that Church until his death ; and that Church has continued a Baptist Church unto this day.

But he belonged to the *Advance Guard.* He was a *true liberal* in Church fellowship, and, in consequence, he was viewed by many of the leading Baptists of his day, much in the same light, and with the same feeling of alarm, as that in which an honest and consistent " Tory " regards a " Radical " in politics.

Baptists were the pioneers of liberty of conscience, as touching the different sections of the Church ; and he among Baptists was the pioneer of that liberty of conscience extended to individual faith and practice.

He held, that as evident faith in Christ makes a man a member of Christ, so also it should place him on a full equality with Christ's other members of His body, which is the Church. And therefore he admitted into Church fellowship all who gave evidence of faith, without respect to baptism, leaving that as a matter for further instruction and light. In his " Reason for my practice in Worship," he says—" Touching shadowish or figurative ordinances I believe that Christ hath ordained but two in His Church, viz., Water-Baptism and the Supper of the Lord : both which are of excellent use to the Church in this world—they being to us representations of the death and resurrection of Christ—and are, as God shall make them, helps to our faith. But I count them not the fundamentals of our Christianity, nor grounds or rule to communion with saints : servants they are, and our mystical ministers, to teach and instruct us in the most weighty matters of the Kingdom of God. I therefore here declare my reverent esteem for them, yet dare not remove them, as some do, from the place and end where by God they are set and appointed ; nor ascribe unto them more than they were ordered to have in their first and primitive institution. It is possible to commit idolatry even with God's own appointments. The Church must first look to faith, then to good living, according to the ten commandments ; after that she must respect those appointments of our Lord Jesus, that respect her outward order and discipline, and then she walks as becomes her—sinning if she neglecteth either, sinning if she overvalueth either."

In answer to the question as to with whom he would hold communion, and by what rule he would gather persons into Church fellowship, he says, " I dare to have communion, Church communion, with all those who are visible saints by calling," and, " my only rule for their reception is that rule by which they were discovered to the Church to be visible saints, and willing to be gathered into their fellowship.　By that Word of God therefore, by which their faith, experience, and conversation, being examined, is found good ; by that, the Church should receive them into fellowship."

Answering an opponent, he says, " To make Baptism the including and excluding charter, when in the Word of the Everlasting Testament there is no word for it, to speak charitably, if it be not for want of love, it is for want of light.　Strange ! take two Christians equal in all points ; nay, let one go beyond the other in grace and goodness as far as a man is beyond a babe, yet water shall turn the scale, shall open the door of communion to the one, and command the other to stand back."

These opinions are permeating the Baptist body all over the world, and a large number of churches now follow Bunyan's practice.　May the day soon come when the Church's offer of membership shall be as far-reaching as is Christ's offer of salvation, and the only test of membership, Christ's test of faith in Himself !

In all this remarkable life we see the master-hand of the Divine Sculptor, finely chiseling that rude, shapeless block of humanity, and bringing forth feature after feature, until there stands before us a " Jesus Christ's man," a grand model for future generations of preachers and writers.

Let us praise Him Who in such a wondrous way, out of such heathen darkness, produced such a bright and shining light, and out of the blaspheming tinker of Bedford, made the man, who wrote that marvellous description of man's pilgrimage from sin to God, which has been the pole-star to thousands of lost sinners, and will be to generations yet unborn:—a book so simple that the most ignorant can understand it, so interesting that children delight to read it, and withal so grand that the most capable intellects have read and re-read its pages, and have reverently bared their heads to its author's genius.

Young men, if you want character, usefulness, and enduring worth, do as Bunyan did; believe something, be something, do something. Seek Bunyan's God, hold fast to Bunyan's Saviour, and reverently bend your will to His. He Who made the "immortal dreamer" out of such raw material, what can He not make of you, with your larger opportunities and fuller light?

DAN TAYLOR AND THE ENGLISH BAPTISTS,

BY

REV. J. FLETCHER.

———◆———

THE Rev. Dan Taylor was born in 1738, and died in 1816. He was 22 years of age when George II. ceased to reign, and he saw 56 years of the long reign of George III. Dying as he did, in the year after the Battle of Waterloo, he is distinctly remembered by persons now living; but it is for us to remember that the subject of this Lecture belonged not so much to the 19th century as to the England of a hundred years ago. How fondly some people look back to that time! It was the time "when George III. was King;" and what more need be said for it? They were "the good old days." It should not be forgotten, however, that the days referred to were neither so good nor so old as the days in which it is our happiness to live. The material, the intellectual, and the moral advancement which distinguishes the present century, was then unknown, and the spiritual condition of the people was mournful in the extreme. The contrast in all these respects, between that time and this, is very remarkable. Then, they had no gas, and no electric light, but had to make darkness visible by means of candles and oil lamps. They had no penny post, no penny newspapers, no electric telegraph, no telephone; there were no railways, no locomotive engines, and no steam ships.

Macadam had not taught the art of making roads, and in our large cities, asphalte and wood paving were unknown. Dick Turpin is almost a legendary character to the youth of our land, so strangely do his exploits strike on modern ears, and yet that notorious highwayman flourished in England little more than a hundred years ago. He was executed the year after Dan Taylor was born, but for years after his death, deeds of robbery and violence were so common, that travellers went armed at mid-day as though they were going to a battle.

Profane swearing was the constant practice of the higher classes at that time. It was to be heard everywhere. Ladies swore in their drawing-rooms ; Navy Chaplains swore at the sailors ; Judges swore in our Courts of Law ; and the King swore in the Royal Palace. A single anecdote will reveal the habit of the time better, perhaps, than any lengthened statement. Lord Campbell mentions a call made by the Duchess of Marlborough, in 1738, on William Murray, afterwards Lord Mansfield. Murray was not in: the lady declined to leave her name, but the clerk in describing who had called, said, "I could not make out, sir, who she was, but she swore so dreadfully, that she must be a lady of quality." Another evil of that time was the passion for gin-drinking, which infected the masses of the people like a plague. Gin was cheap. The retailers of that spirit hung out painted boards announcing that persons could be made drunk for a penny, dead drunk for two-pence, and be accommodated with clean straw for nothing. The result was a fearful increase in poverty, crime, immorality, disease, and death. Added to this was the wretched state of the law relating to marriage ; no publication of banns was required. Any priest in orders could marry persons at any time and place. Numbers of dissolute clergymen made this their business. The marriages were commonly performed in taverns. Touters stood outside to ask passers-by if they would like to be married, just as they now stand outside the shops of photographers to ask if people will have their portraits taken. "Fleet marriages" they were called, because performed in the vicinity of Fleet Prison, which once stood on the east side of Farringlon Street. One of these Fleet Parsons married 173 couples in a single day. Multitudes were married when they were drunk, and hundreds who were thus united had not seen or known each other more than a few hours.

The criminal law was equally bad. Our prisons were so badly kept that a malignant disease called jail fever broke out in them. At the present time only one crime is punishable with death, but in 1765 there were over two hundred offences to which that penalty was attached. Executions were a favourite public spectacle. It was a very ordinary thing to see ten or twelve culprits all hung at the same time.

E lucation was in the same unsatisfactory condition. It was a mockery to speak of the Universities as "Seats of learning ;" and as for the common people, they were sunk in an ignorance so deplorable, that down in Somersetshire a Methodist preacher was actually brought before a Magistrate and charged with swearing, because he had quoted in a sermon the words :—" He that believeth not shall be damned." In fact, until quite recent years, not half the children of the land were sent to school, and not half the mothers of those children could write their own names.

The state of religion was simply lamentable. Both Conformists and Non-conformists had become cold and dead. The land was almost destitute of vital religion, as Bishop Butler and Joseph Addison both testify. The habit of extemporaneous preaching had almost died out. Vast numbers of the parochial Clergy knew more of hunting, shooting, swearing, drinking, and gambling, than they did of the Gospel. With rare exceptions, the highest aim of the best of them was simply to make men moral. So little was there of real Gospel preaching, that Blackstone, the learned author of the " Commentaries on the Laws of England," said, after hearing every clergyman of note in London, that from no single discourse could he discover whether the preacher were a follower of Confucius, of Mahomet, or of Christ"; and Berridge, of Everton, speaking of the same time, said, in his odd but striking way, that "an angel might preach such doctrine as was commonly preached till his wings dropped off, without doing any good."

Such were the times in which Dan Taylor spent his earlier years. They were times to call loudly for holy and earnest men, but they were hardly the times to call *forth* such men. Yet how often has it been observed that "When things are at the worst they mend." An old Jewish proverb says :—"When the tale of bricks is doubled, then comes Moses." Even so, when the spiritual needs of England were greatest, God raised up a triumvirate of deliverers in the persons of John and Charles Wesley, and George Whitfield. The highest place must always be accorded to these three men when speaking of the religious revival of the last century. But they were not the only men. In the time of David there were three mighty men, but besides these there were thirty others who were heroes of the second rank, an l among the thirty was Benaiah, who was more honourable than all the rest, and worthy to be named with the first three, although he was not actually among them. (2 Sam. xxiii. 23.) It was like that in the 18th century. Spiritual hero, as Dan Taylor certainly was, and anxious as I am to do full justice to his worth, it would be folly in me to give him a place which impartial history has not given him. Dan Taylor is known by his thousands, but the Wesleys and Whitfield are known by their tens of thousands. I cannot therefore claim for my hero a place in the front rank, but I can and do claim for him a distinguished place among the heroes of the rank of Benaiah. He was more honourable than his compeers, though he "attained not to the first three."

Having looked at the time in which Dan Taylor lived, and having glanced at his relation to the religious reformers of that time, let us now turn to the man himself, and to the consideration of his life and work.

The paternal grandfather of Dan Taylor was born in 1650. He was a farmer of good repute, was twice married, and had 22 children. Six of these he lost in a single fortnight through the ravages of small pox. Adam Taylor did not name his children out of his own experience as Brewster, one of the Pilgrim Fathers did, calling one Wrestling, another Fear, a third Patience, and a fourth Love. He seems rather to have named them out of the Scriptures ; for the six just referred to were called respectively— Tamar, Terah, Zara, Er, Abiah, and Tirzah. The 20th child in this large family had also a Scripture name. He was called Azor. In fact the entire record is so much after the Bible fashion that I cannot do better than give the genealogy in Scripture phrase and say, Adam begat Azor, and Azor begat Dan.

Dan was born on December 21st, 1738, at Sour-milk Hall, in the parish of Northowram, near Halifax, in the West Riding of Yorkshire. Sour-milk Hall, as I remember it, from having seen it scores of times in my own boyhood, had the appearance of an ancient mansion. Like another building, called Scout Hall, not far away from it, in the beautiful Vale of Shibden, it retained its ancient name long after it had been divided into tenements. Plas Mawr, or the Great Mansion, which is shown to visitors at Conway, in Wales, has undergone a similar change. The home was a very humble one, for the father of Dan Taylor, like the father of Martin Luther, was only a working miner. Here the child grew and increased in knowledge. At the age of three he could read well, and before he was five years of age he was famed for being able to read that "hard chapter," the 10th of Nehemiah. At Church, the clergyman, struck with his ability, inquired, "Who taught you to read, my boy?" Dan proudly and loudly replied, "My mother, sir." As to the rest of his education we may adopt the answer given of Charles Dickens by his father, who said, "Why indeed, sir, he may· be said to have educated himself." It was well for Dan that he learned to read so early, for we are told, incredible as it may seem, that "when almost five years of age" he had to go down and work with his father in the darkness of a coal-mine some 300 feet deep. It was a common thing in those days for little children to labour in the mines from 14 to 16 hours a day. Their work was to drag away the corves, or little waggons, which the pitmen had filled with coal. This they did by means of a chain fastened round the waist, and sometimes the poor little fellows had to crawl on hands and feet in order to drag the heavy load. If this occupation retarded the growth of Dan, it does not appear to have otherwise injured his vigorous frame, and however much it diminished his opportunities, it did not in the least diminish his thirst for knowledge. Difficulty added zest to his pursuit of learning. He carried books down into the mine, and in spite of the coal-dust, he improved the candle-light of those grim caverns by occasional snatches of reading.

Once whilst engaged in the mine he had a remarkable escape from death. An immense volume of water burst, without warning, through a thin partition of coal, and quickly flooded the pit to the height of several fathoms. Before the collier with whom he was working could rise to his feet, Dan leapt over his body, and ran faster than the rushing water to the bottom of the shaft, and was at once drawn up to the surface. It was afterwards found that the man was also saved in an equally marvellous manner. An event of a very different kind made a most lasting and salutary impression on the mind of the young miner. When only nine years of age he was accidentally struck with a pickaxe, and having a passionate temper, he began to swear at the striker. His father, hearing of the circumstance, flogged him most severely, but he mingled with the chastisement such expostulation and warning as the lad never forgot. Among other things the father reminded him in solemn tones of these words, "The great day of His wrath is come and who shall be able to stand?" Thirty-five years afterwards, when that godly father was in his coffin, the son preached his funeral sermon from the same words, and confessed that a correction so solemn had carried to his soul the conviction of sin.

As they grew up it was the rare privilege of Dan and his
brother John to hear the preaching of Whitfield and the two
Wesleys, and it was their meat and drink to trudge 20 or 30 miles
on such an errand.   But the preacher Dan liked best was the
Rev. Wm. Grimshaw, of Haworth, a place since celebrated as the
abode of Charlotte Brontë and her sisters.   Haworth was a wild,
outlandish place, 12 miles away from Halifax, but Dan felt amply
repaid for walking that distance if he could only hear Mr. Grimshaw.   Hundreds did and felt the same.   Mr. Grimshaw was a
wonderful man.   During his ministry at Haworth the communi-
cants increased from 12 to 1200.   He was a plain preacher, spoke
"market language," and was intensely fervent.   Regardless of
parish bounds, he scoured the country for miles round, and
frequently preached from 20 to 30 times a week.   He was a terror
to evil-doers.   At his approach, those who were drinking in
public-houses would flee out of the back-doors and windows to
escape his admonitions.   Many anecdotes are told of his eccentric
ways, but one will show the sterling worth of the man.   The
Archbishop appointed a confirmation at his church.   When the
day arrived the clergy and laity assembled in great numbers.
Before the service the Archbishop said, "I have heard many
extraordinary reports respecting your conduct, Mr. Grimshaw,
how you preach in private houses in other parishes than your
own, and that in fact you can and do preach about anything.
That I may judge for myself, I shall expect you to preach before
me and the clergy present in two hours hence, from the text I am
about to name."   He named the text and gave Mr. Grimshaw
leave to retire while he confirmed the young people.   Mr. Grimshaw, looking at the assembled multitude, replied, "My Lord,
why keep them out of the sermon for two hours?   Send a clergyman to read prayers, and I will begin immediately."   The
Archbishop did so.   Mr. Grimshaw ascended the pulpit, and so
prayed and wrestled with God for the Archbishop and people, that
the congregation, the clergy, and the Archbishop himself, were

moved to tears. After the sermon, the Archbishop took him by
the hand, and turning to those who stood near, said, "I would to
God that all the clergy in my diocese were like this good man."
How much of Mr. Grimshaw's spirit was caught by Dan Taylor
will appear by and by. Meanwhile he attached himself to the
Methodists. At prayer meetings and class meetings he was often
in deep anguish of soul, till at last the light came through the
beautiful window in John iii. 16, " God so loved the world," &c.—
words which have led thousands to Christ and His salvation. In
his twentieth year he formally joined the Wesleyan Society, and
was soon thrust forth to preach. Thrust forth, for when he had declined frequent invitations, the Superintendent of the circuit
ended the matter by informing him one evening that he must
preach early next morning before a select company of judges.
This intimation came upon Dan so suddenly, and at the same
time so coolly, that to refuse was out of the question. He retired
to his lodging, and there by the light of the fire sat up the greater
part of the night preparing for the ordeal. His sermon was
delivered from Eph. ii. 8, "By grace are ye saved." The preacher
stepped down from the pulpit very much ashamed of his work,
but the judges felt otherwise, and he was at once placed on probation as a local preacher.

No sooner had this sturdy coal-miner begun to preach than
his friends advised him to apply to Mr. Wesley for an appointment in the itinerant ministry. This Mr. Taylor declined to do.
He had no objection to the Methodists on the ground of doctrine,
for like them he was a decided Arminian, but he was too jealous
of his rights as an individual Christian, and too independent in
spirit to be kept bound under the oligarchy of Methodism.
In company with others, three of whom became Calvinistic
ministers, Mr. Taylor seceded from the Wesleyan body. A few
others, like minded with himself, had previously taken the same
course. These resided in a village nine miles from Halifax, in
the township adjoining Heptonstall. It was a hilly district,

where pastureland and moorland blended with each other, and
where the wildness of nature was visibly retreating before the
advancing foot of civilization. The inhabitants were scattered,
ignorant, and depraved. Mr. Taylor knew but four Christians in
the place. At their invitation he entered the ministry. He
preached for them in the summer-time under a tree, in the open
air, at a place called the Nook, in Wadsworth. Not one man in
a thousand would dream of entering the ministry under circumstances so repellant. There was no place for preaching except the
place just named; there were none to render him support save
a mere handful of poor people without means or influence; in
fact there was nothing whatever to tempt him to such a sphere
but the opportunity for self-sacrifice in preaching the Gospel.
But let it be said, to the eternal honour of Dan Taylor, that
throughout the whole of his long career he never sought for self.
The opportunity for self-denial in the cause of Christ was all he
ever craved, and all he ever got.

At Michaelmas, 1762, he bade farewell to the coal mine and
settled in this unpromising region. At the approach of winter, a
room was taken for the double purpose of week day teaching, and
Lord's day preaching, Mr. Taylor's earnings in the former occupation helping to support him in the latter. Having found a local
habitation, the assembled Christians wanted a name. They had
seceded from Methodism without considering what they should
become. They were only prevented from joining the Independents
by a difference of opinion as to the extent of the atonement. A
double difference kept them at that time from joining the Particular
Baptists. The term "Particular," spoke of particular redemption,
whereas Mr. Taylor and his friends believed that Jesus Christ
tasted death for *every* man. The term "Baptists" spoke of the
immersion of believers, and that was a doctrine which Mr. Taylor
had no wish to believe. But when the question came up among
the members of his small community, he felt bound to study it.
The study made him a Baptist in spite of himself, and, strange to

say, it was the most learned work he could find on the Pædo-Baptist side (Dr. Wall's History of Infant Baptism) that "contributed more than any other book, except the New Testament, to convince him that infant baptism has no foundation in Scripture, but is wholly an invention of man." Mr. Taylor's friends were neither Epicureans nor Stoics. None of them said, "may we know what this new doctrine is?" Nevertheless he told them. One by one they embraced the same view, and wanted to put on Christ in baptism. How were they to obtain baptism? Their minister was himself unbaptized, and under the circumstances, he hesitated to baptize any of the rest. Who baptized John the Baptist, or whether he ever was baptized, none can tell; but among these people it was felt that he who baptized others should first seek baptism for himself. This Mr. Taylor assayed to do, but can you believe it in this 19th century? Because he believed that Christ died for the sins of the whole world, no Particular Baptist minister would baptize him. Of any other Baptists Mr. Taylor and his friends knew nothing. They were hardly likely to know anything about the small sect called Six Principle Baptists, whose distinguishing tenets are contained in Heb. vi. 1, 2, viz., repentance, faith, baptism, the laying on of hands, the resurrection of the dead, and eternal judgment. Still less were they likely to know anything about the Seventh-day Baptists, who worship on the Jewish Sabbath, for these have never been numerous in this country, and but two congregations exist in England, I believe, at the present time. The Scotch Baptists, with their weekly observance of the Lord's Supper, their plurality of elders in every Church, their love feast, kiss of charity, washing of one another's feet, and abstinence from things strangled and from blood, had not yet come into existence.

At length Mr. Taylor heard of the oldest Baptists in the country—the General Baptists. He was told that at Boston, in Lincolnshire, there was a minister of the same faith as himself, who would probably be glad to baptize him. To Boston, therefore, he

H

must go. The distance was 120 miles, and the place could only be reached on foot. In company with John Slater, Mr. Taylor set out on this long journey. The winter was at its worst. The water was out in many places, and at the close of the first day's journey, the hapless travellers found themselves in a field surrounded by floods. The darkness prevented their escape ; and the two candidates for baptism were compelled to sleep all night under the shelter of a haystack. Rising early to pursue their journey, the next night found them at a place eight miles beyond Gamston, near Retford. Learning that some General Baptists existed at Gamston, they returned to that village the next day, which was Sunday, and entered the quaint old chapel, which has recently given way to a new one. Mr. Dossey, the minister, gave them a hearty welcome, and introduced them to his colleague, Mr. Jeffrey. The father of Mr. Jeffrey founded the cause at this place, while in the service of the Earl of Clare ; and it is worthy of remark that he had obtained a situation under the noble Earl, simply and solely on the confession—" I am a General Baptist." The Gamston friends treated the inquirers with every hospitality. Two or three days were spent in converse with the ministers, and on Wednesday, Feb. 16th, 1763, Dan Taylor was baptized in the river Idle, by Mr. Jeffrey.

Eager to know more of this denomination, and finding that the Lincolnshire Association of General Baptists would meet at Boston in the following May, Mr. Taylor resolved to be present. Arriving at the appointed time, he found the chair occupied by the Rev. Gilbert Boyce, who was messenger of the Churches. This office is still preserved, in name at least, by the General Baptist Assembly. One writer describes it as " an episcopacy, a presbytery, and an inquisition all in one." By Grantham the Messengers are styled "Subordinate Apostles of Christ." Here Mr. Taylor made the acquaintance of the Rev. W. Thompson, of Boston, the minister he had set out to see in February, and a life-long friendship sprang up between them. Mr. Thompson went back with him into

Yorkshire, formed the fourteen members at Wadsworth into a Church, and on a subsequent visit, when accompanied by Messrs. Boyce of Coningsby, and Dossey of Gamston, Mr. Taylor was ordained.

Soon after this event a new Chapel was projected. A site was purchased on the steep hill-side called Birchcliffe, near Hebden Bridge. The Chapel was to cost £140, a formidable sum in those days to that people. To raise the money Mr. Taylor travelled, on one occasion, into the five Shires of Derby, Leicester, Northampton, Rutland, and Nottingham : preached thirty-four times, and took home £22. To raise the building he was "in labours more abundant." He bought the timber and engaged the builder. He was by turns architect, quarryman, over-looker, and clerk of the works : and when the building was finished he crowned his labours by carrying the pulpit on his back from the old meeting house to the new.

Soon after his acquaintance with the Lincolnshire General Baptists, Mr. Taylor found to his regret that anti-evangelical sentiments had taken deep root among them. They were fast becoming Unitarians. Mr. Taylor tried long and hard to bring them back to his own views, but all in vain. He must try another course. In the Midland Counties Mr. Taylor had discovered some General Baptists whose sentiments were as evangelical as his own. Their head centre was Barton-in-the-Beans, a small hamlet near to where Richard III., the last of the Plantagenets, met his death at the battle of Bosworth Field. Between these unassociated Churches, and the Churches of the Assembly, Mr. Taylor sought to form a union, in the hope that the new leaven would purge out the old. This attempt also failed. There was no alternative but to attempt the formation of a new connexion. The venerable Gilbert Boyce did all he could to prevent the secession, and had the reasons for withdrawal been less serious than they were, he might have succeeded. It was no personal question, no mere struggle for supremacy, no friction in the machinery which a little oil would remove : to Mr. Taylor's mind it was a battle for God's Truth. "It is not to be doubted," said he, "if we regard the Bible, that some of the vilest errors are, in this age, maintained by some of the General Baptists, with as much warmth as they have ever been by any party of men in former ages. It behoves us therefore to take the alarm, and with all the little might we have to militate against those pernicious tenets which our forefathers so much abhorred, and which the Word of God so expressly con-demns." That these were the only reasons for the step Mr. Taylor took, is abundantly evident from the friendly relations he long sustained, both to individuals in the Assembly and to the Assembly itself.

I need not discuss the preliminary steps which were necessary to start the new denomination. Suffice it that on June 6th, 1770, Mr. Taylor met his friends at Mr. Brittain's Meeting-House, Church Lane, Whitechapel, that on the following morning he delivered a discourse from the words "Be not thou ashamed of the testimony of the Lord," that in the afternoon he was called to the chair, and that six Articles of Faith which Mr. Taylor had prepared, were read, approved, and signed by the nineteen ministers present, (himself included), that the Churches represented numbered 1,635 members, and that the name by which they called themselves was, The Assembly of Free Grace General Baptists. Thus sprang into being, what is now called the General Baptist Association, or in other words the New Connexion of General Baptists.

Mr. Taylor at this time was exceedingly popular as a preacher, and indefatigable as a worker. He cultivated his gifts with untiring toil. Usually he rose at five and went to bed at ten, but many a time and oft his growing labours compelled him to sit up half the night. He read incessantly and systematically, theology, history, biography, and philosophy, and kept up an acquaintance with mathematics, Greek, and Latin. His recreation he found in his work. He preached, on an average, six times a week the year through. Having preached in the morning and afternoon at

Birchcliffe, he would set off across the wild and rugged country to Queenshead (now Queensbury), to Shore, to Halifax, to Worsthorn, or to Burnley. At Worsthorn some "lewd fellows of the baser sort," threatened to drag him from the pulpit, and one of them rose during the service and moved forward with that intent, but the preacher eyed him with a look so stedfast that he relinquished his purpose before reaching the pulpit stairs. The distance to Burnley was fourteen miles, and it was generally two o'clock in the morning before he got back home. In several of these places he was the means of building Chapels, and in all he made himself responsible for the regular preaching of the Gospel. In addition to all this, it was his habit to make frequent excursions on foot among all the Churches of the denomination, preaching every day. After a fortnight's work of this kind, among the Midland Churches, he took home £70 towards the new Chapel at Queenshead. During the year in which the Chapel at Halifax was being built, he made seven of these excursions in order to aid the work. When the Church complained of his frequent absence, he made what amends he could by training local preachers to fill his vacant pulpit.

In order to provide things honourable in the sight of all men, he added to his school a shop, but this not succeeding, he sold off the goods and took a farm, and at the same time began a boarding school, which soon numbered fourteen boarders and about thirty other pupils. Amid all these labours he found opportunity to publish in rhyme an answer to a Socinian pamphlet by the celebrated Dr. Priestley of Leeds. He also published a Catechism, which during his life-time went through about eleven editions. He subsequently published an " Essay on the Right Use of Earthly Treasure ;" and dealt with that delicate subject in a manner and in a spirit which would have delighted the soul of John Wesley. But his great work, his *chef-d'œuvre*, originally published in 1775, was the " Fundamentals ;" or, " Principal parts of the Christian Religion in Faith and Practice." It is a plain but solid work permeated with Scripture truth, and it remains to this day the best volume of its class in General Baptist Literature.

His habit of treating texts was quite puritanical. One of his sermons delivered at an Ordination, had three main divisions, forty-four sub-divisions, and six reasons for enforcing the foregoing, making fifty-three in all. But the charge delivered to his brother John as pastor at Queenshead was the most extraordinary of all. No wonder his brother deemed it both "long and heavy," for one of the hearers said it contained 600 particulars. His usual plan in preparing for the pulpit was to compose notes and outlines, these would frequently contain a score of particulars. He seldom used them in preaching, but placed them between the leaves of his Bible to be used if needful.

Mr. Taylor was also a master in debate. He was fearless as Luther. When the young and gifted minister of the church at Kegworth began to teach Socinian errors, and when four neighbouring ministers had failed in public discussion to convince him of his error, Mr. Taylor was sent for. He went. A public discussion was agreed upon between himself and the Kegworth pastor, which took place in the chapel at Castle Donington. On the appointed day the building was crowded to excess. The fate of all the churches far and near seemed to hang upon that discussion. The debate lasted for ten hours, from 10 a.m. to 8 p.m., and was attended with the most satisfactory results. The heresy was checked, the cause of evangelical truth triumphed : then had the churches rest throughout all the denomination.

Some time after this event Mr. Taylor received a call from the Church at Halifax, his native town, to be their minister. "Of course," you will say, "it was for more money." On the contrary, it was for less. True, Halifax was the most flourishing town in all that district, but the cause at Haley Hill (since transferred to North Parade) was in its infancy. That, however, was not the main difficulty. The removal of an ordained minister from his sphere of labour was an unknown thing in the denomination, and the spirit of the time was against it. Mr. Taylor would neither say yes nor no. After the Association and several Conferences had been consulted, the matter was left to "the decision of Providence," which was that Mr. Taylor should go to Halifax for six months, while another minister should take his place at Birchcliffe, in order to see how the change would be likely to work. The experiment was successful. His people at Birchcliffe were constrained to part with him, but it was a fine tribute to their pastor's worth when they said it was "one of the greatest troubles they had ever known."

Mr. Taylor was now 45 years of age, and what with a family of seven young children, and a small Church, meeting in a heavily burdened chapel, he had hard work to live. Nevertheless he threw himself into his work with unwonted energy. He preached three times on Sundays, the Lord "confirming the word with signs following." One notable instance of this occurred in the case of an Irishman, Patrick Phelon by name, who had been a Roman Catholic and a soldier. This man, who had no sympathy whatever with the "Dippers," was induced one Sunday morning to hear Mr. Taylor preach. He went also in the afternoon, and again in the evening. In the morning he learned that he was not a child of God ; in the afternoon he heard the way of salvation ; and in the evening he adopted Joshua's resolution to serve the Lord. The resolution thus formed he kept by the grace of God to the end of life, and when he came to die, the doctor was so impressed with his conversation that he said, " I never before had such a patient —he knows the way to heaven ! "

In addition to his home work, Mr. Taylor, in order to reduce the chapel debt, resorted to his usual method of visiting the churches near and far, preaching and collecting money. Mounted on his pony he rode sixty miles one day, and fifty-five the next, preached in London the same night, and then wrote that "after very great fatigue, he and his pony were in good spirits." Towards the close of another excursion he came to Epworth in Lincolnshire. On the Friday he baptised some candidates, and preached three times. On the Saturday he started for home. It was a "frightful journey." He rode on a borrowed galloway twenty-four miles, and walked thirty-eight more amid rain and mire. He went to bed, and on the following day preached three times, held three other meetings between the services, and, to use his own words, got through the whole "with moderate ease and pleasure."

So passionately did he prosecute his work, that before he was 47 years of age, this zealous pastor, this ardent home missionary, this successor to labours, if not to endowments, apostolic, had travelled, preaching the Gospel and confirming the churches, no less a distance than 25,000 miles, or more than the entire circuit of the globe.

Mr. Taylor had been only two years at Halifax when he was invited to London. The Society of General Baptists, meeting at Church Lane, Whitechapel, had existed from the time of Oliver Cromwell and the early years of the Commonwealth. Its foundation is ascribed to Samuel Loveday. The Church Lane Chapel, a plain brick building, was opened in 1763. It was relinquished for Beulah, now called Commercial Road, Chapel, in 1821. In 1770, the Church numbered about 300 members, but in fourteen years the numbers had declined to 150. The aged pastor, Mr. Brittain, felt the need of help. Mr. Taylor was invited. The invitation reached him as he was following the plough. He knew not how to decide, nor did any of his friends know what to advise. The question agitated the whole Connexion for twelve months. At length the matter was left to the decision of the Association, and, after a ten hours' discussion, it was agreed " that it would be most for the glory of God for Brother Taylor to remove to London." Selling off his farming stock, his furniture, and most of his books, Mr. Taylor left Yorkshire for London, with his wife and nine children, on July 21st, 1785. Their mode of travelling was as primitive as that which characterised the removal of the patriarch Jacob into Egypt, for this journey, like that, was accomplished by means of a waggon lent for the purpose. The distance was 217 miles, and after eight days' riding, the whole family arrived safely at their new home, Turville Street, Cock Lane, Spitalfields.

What he would want in London with such a family Mr. Taylor did not know. What the Church offered him was £100 a year. Meat was cheaper then than it is now, but wheat, which for a few years was at its present value, gradually rose in price, till in the year 1801 the quartern loaf was sold for a time at one shilling and tenpence. Mr. Taylor's friends thought him exceedingly venture-some in coming to London for so small a salary, but they consoled themselves and comforted him, by saying, that he was " so hard, as to be able to get though anything that could be gotten through."

As co-pastor with Mr. Brittain, Mr. Taylor undertook the preaching almost entirely. The congregations increased and many were added to the Church. Nor were the claims of a London pastorate allowed to interfere with his former practice of preaching the Gospel in the regions beyond. " The care of all the churches " was upon him. They looked up to him as their chief adviser and friend. In short, he was like Ahithophel of old: "the counsel which he counselled was as if a man inquired at the oracle of God." He had mentioned the claims and expectations of other churches to the people at Church Lane, as a reason why they should not invite him ; but they, anxious to obtain his services upon almost any terms, promised him " full liberty respecting his journeys." In London, as in previous spheres, he became engaged in various controversies. One of them was about *singing*. This important and delightful feature in Divine worship was once considered a dangerous and unscriptural innovation. Volumes have been written about it, both for and against. Thomas Gran-tham said, that more could be urged " for all praying at once than for all singing at once." The solo-singing revived of late years by Mr. Sankey, was once regarded as more scriptural than con-gregational singing. The singing of "rhymes by set-form, by all the people together, whether saints or sinners, members or no members," was described by Dr. Russell, in 1696, as a "mere human invention of *ballad-singing.*" At Bristol a congregation was divided on this subject—half of them liked singing, and half of them were opposed to it. Those who disliked it, gravely asked permission, if this thing were practised, either to *keep on their hats*, or to *go out* during that part of the service. At Church Lane the practise had been introduced very cautiously. It began, in 1722, with one hymn at each service, and it was seven years later before they ventured to sing after the sermon. The old General Baptists held out against the practice in Mr. Taylor's time, and its revival in the New Connexion moved the venerable Gilbert Boyce to publish "Serious Thoughts" upon it. He also wrote to Mr. Taylor a very severe letter on the subject. Thus challenged, Mr. Taylor replied in a pamphlet, entitled, "A Dissertation on Singing in the Worship of God," in which he gave advice, replied to objections, and vindicated the practice of the New Connexion churches.

With the Rev. Andrew Fuller, of Kettering, he had a controversy of a more formidable character. Mr. Fuller published a pamphlet, entitled, "The Gospel Worthy of all Acceptation : or, the Obligation of Men fully to credit and cordially to approve whatever God makes known." Under that title Mr. Fuller claimed to make free use of the universal calls of Scripture, whilst at the same time he held the doctrines of election and particular redemption. The high Calvinists were alarmed at his concessions ; the more moderate of them rejoiced that he yielded so much ; the Arminians were sorry he did not yield more. At the urgent request of several friends, Mr. Taylor published a reply in the shape of "Nine Letters to a Friend : " by *Philanthropos.* In those letters Mr. Taylor took the ground that the Gospel ought indeed to be preached to every man, and that every man ought to believe it for the simple and sufficient reason that Christ had made an atonement for the sins of all mankind. Mr. Fuller published a rejoinder, and Mr. Taylor followed with another reply, to which he subscribed his name. Some three years afterwards, a pamphlet was issued from the press, bearing the following title, " The Reality and Efficacy of Divine Grace ; with the certain success of Christ's Sufferings on behalf of all who are finally saved : considered in a Series of Letters to the Rev. Andrew Fuller : containing remarks on the observations of the Rev. Dan Taylor, on Mr. Fuller's reply to Philanthropos. By *Agnostos.*"

A prominent Baptist minister, a friend of Mr. Fuller, was thought to be the writer. People were confirmed in this view by the fact that the letters praised Mr. Fuller very highly. Years afterwards it was discovered that Agnostos, who wrote the letters *to* Mr. Fuller, was none other than Mr. Fuller himself. Mr. Taylor published a " Friendly Conclusion," and the subject forthwith dropped. There is no need to claim the victory for one side over the other. Suffice it, that the concessions made by Mr. Fuller exhibit a wide departure from the old Calvinism, and make a very near approach to Arminianism ; and that the discussion secured what Mr. Taylor had at heart, viz., a wider, freer, and more earnest proclamation of the everlasting Gospel.

The ink shed over this controversy was scarcely dry when Mr. Taylor had to attack a doctrine which has found new advocates in recent years—I mean the doctrine of Universal Restoration. Its promoter at that time was the Rev. Elkanah Winchester, from America, and Mr. Taylor, at the double request of the Rev. Abraham Booth, and a clergyman of the Established Church, prepared and printed a reply. Referring to that reply some seventeen years after its publication, the Rev. Dr. Winter pronounced it so forcible, so judicious, and so complete, as to leave nothing to be desired. His busy pen and busier brain had little or no rest. He sent to the press a work on Baptism, which went through seven editions. He also issued a volume on the " Truth and Inspiration of the Holy Scriptures." So large a share did he take in compiling the first General Baptist Hymn-book, that it was frequently called by his name. He also commenced, and conducted for three years, the first General Baptist Magazine.

Amid these varied labours, affliction entered his home. His wife and three daughters were all ill at one time with scarlet fever ; and such was the devotion of the husband and father, that for six weeks he never took off his clothes, except to change them. Worn with constant anxiety, he was himself seized with rheumatism and an affliction of the eyes. Embarrassment trod on the heels of affliction, and to increase his slender salary he opened a bookseller's shop in Union Street, Bishopsgate Street. Then came the heaviest blow of all, in the loss of her who for twenty-nine years had been to him a most devoted wife. Mrs. Taylor died, leaving nine children out of a family of thirteen. Immediately after this painful bereavement, the Rev. W. Thompson, of Boston, his intimate and valued friend, was taken away. Mr. Brittain, his aged colleague in the ministry, soon followed. Then came a severe personal affliction, in the form of a burning fever, and an ulcerated sore throat. This laid him aside from his pulpit for the first time in his whole ministry of more than thirty years. It was in the month of February, 1795. The buoyancy of his nature soon threw off the disease, and the summer found him as busy as ever. On one of his excursions he preached fourteen times in the space of a fortnight. At home he composed five or six sermons a week, and only complained because he had not much time left for general reading.

In 1797, at a time of life when many men lay down their work, Mr. Taylor entered upon a new and responsible undertaking. He had long wished to see established an institution for the training of young ministers ; and even when in Wadsworth he had taken one or two young men into his house for that purpose. At last the Association resolved to open an Academy, and Mr. Taylor was earnestly asked to become the Tutor. He accepted the office, and served in it both faithfully and usefully for fifteen years, performing at the same time his duties as a pastor, and combining with both a remarkable amount of other labour.

The memorable language of the 90th Psalm runs thus : " The days of our years are threescore years and ten ; and if by reason of strength they be fourscore years, yet is their strength labour and sorrow : for it is soon cut off, and we fly away." When past the age of 70, Mr. Taylor had much strength, and even at the age of 76 he journeyed long distances and preached to crowded congregations almost every day. Yet was his labour mingled with sorrow. His Church was sadly weakened by internal dissensions. His slender income was reduced one third ; and the building of a house for the better accommodation of his family and students, almost brought him to financial ruin. Just then his second wife, who had been an "unspeakable blessing" to himself, his family, and the Church, for more than fifteen years, was taken away. After a period of eighteen months he married a third time, but he found it far easier to please himself than to satisfy his Church, even though he married a deacon's daughter. At the age of 78, having lost his third wife, he married again, and this time all approved his choice.

At intervals, during the last years of his life, he had suffered from various illnesses, and at length the end came. He had preached twice on the Sunday ; had been out to tea on the Monday, but in the night was restless, and felt some pain. On Tuesday he relished his dinner, after which, as his manner was, he took his pipe and began to read. Suddenly, without any warning, the pipe fell from his hand, his eyes closed, and "he was not, for God took him." His funeral was performed according to his own wish, without *hearse,* or *coach,* or *escutcheon.* He was buried in the ancient burial-ground of Bunhill Fields, on Dec. the 5th, 1816, and strangers, his own people, and the whole denomination mourned for him.

To do anything like justice to Mr. Taylor's various qualities, and to set out fully all his immense labours, would require not a brief lecture but a large volume. But I think I have said enough to show that Dan Taylor was a man of no ordinary type. Under the average height, he was what Tennyson would call

"A square-set man and honest."

He wore a fine grey wig. His portrait may be seen in the well-known engraving of contemporary ministers, published many years ago, and I venture to say, that amid Carey, Knibb, Rippon, Ryland, John Foster, and Robt. Hall, no finer face is found. He had little or no humour, but was sustained in a sea of troubles by a cheerfulness which never failed. In his time he had been collier, schoolmaster, quarryman, architect, shopkeeper, farmer, preacher, poet, controversialist, editor, and Tutor of the College. With the exception of a single year, he was President of the Association from the time of its foundation to the day of his death. He preached before the Association almost as often, and wrote nearly twenty of its Circular Letters. He took part in thirty-eight ordinations, giving the charge in each case either to the pastor or to the Church. He was also present at 200 conferences, wrote forty books, and preached 20,000 sermons.

If genius be a capacity for plodding, he had genius. Of the capacities with which he was endowed he made the most. He had, moreover, a zeal which is better than ability. Napoleon once wrote saying that he enjoyed studying the position of his armies, "like a school-girl her romance." Like Napoleon, but in a very different sphere, Mr. Taylor enjoyed his work. He loved his Bible dearly, and in a portrait, taken when he was 71 years of age, he is represented as clasping the New Testament to his breast with a firmness of grip and a stedfastness of look, as if the very picture were saying :—

"Should all the forms that men devise
Assault my faith with treacherous art,
I'd call them vanity and lies,
And bind the gospel to my heart."

To him, a "Thus saith the Lord" was more than all else in

framing a theory or conducting a discussion. Hence he delighted in quoting the conduct of a countryman who, when the preacher kept saying " I think " this, and " I think " that, called out in the midst of the sermon, "What signifies it what thou thinkest? Tell us what God says." Like Wm. Cobbet, he made it a rule to write and to speak so that he might not only be understood, but so that he could not be misunderstood. Having mastered what he professed to teach, he used great boldness of speech ; indeed his boldness in the pulpit and with the pen was but another manifestation of the same determined spirit which characterised all he did. As our poet-laureate would say, he was

> " A strong man :
> For where he fixt his heart, he set his hand
> To do the thing he will'd, and bore it through."

He fought the fight ; he kept the faith ; and what Paul anticipated, he has found, for to-day, beyond a doubt,

> " He wears a truer crown
> Than any wreath that man can weave him."

THE BAPTISTS & MISSIONARY ENTERPRISE;

BY

REV. J. F. JONES.

———◆———

OF the large number of memorable men who lived during the
second half of the last century, by no means the least
conspicuous was William Carey. He was born in 1761, and in the
26th year of his age, being ordained to the pastoral office, became
the minister of the Baptist Church at Moulton, a village in the
county of Northampton.

William Carey was by trade a shoemaker, or, to be more
correct, a cobbler, for it is reported that he made only one pair of
shoes, which, when finished, were much too long, and which he
put right by cutting off the toes and sewing them up again.
Subsequently he became the village schoolmaster, and in this
capacity found employment much more suitable both to his tastes
and abilities. Whether engaged in mending shoes, or in teaching
children, he was a student, chiefly of languages, to the mastery
of which he applied himself with the utmost diligence.

His mind was however occupied for some years with one
overmastering thought. He had ascertained that of the population
of the world, estimated at 731,000,000, not more than 44,000,000,
or about *one-sixteenth*, were Protestants ; whilst 420,000,000, considerably more than one-half of the entire human race, were

pagans. This fact haunted him continually, and being convinced that the religion of Christ alone could satisfy and save mankind, he conceived the idea of planting the Gospel in heathen lands, and was impelled by an irresistible passion to carry it out.

Having repeatedly consulted his personal friends on the subject, he ventured to raise the question at a meeting of Baptist ministers. From them he received no encouragement ; few sympathised with him ; none were prepared to support him. They declared "the time had not come," "the denomination would not concur in the undertaking," and, above all, that "there was quite sufficient work to be done at home." Though somewhat disappointed, he was by no means daunted. He could think and speak of nothing else, and in a most excellent sense, he became "a man of one idea."

At one of these ministerial meetings presided over by Mr. Ryland, it was suggested that one of the younger brethren should propose a topic for discussion. After a few moment's silence, Carey rose. No question of theological debate did he suggest, but the one question which was always uppermost in his mind, "*the duty of Christians to attempt to spread the Gospel among heathen nations.*" The meeting was thrown into consternation, not another dared to speak save the Chairman, who, with unrestrained vehemence, denounced the young man as an enthusiast.

Being thus treated when he spoke, Carey determined to fight his battle with the pen, and he issued a pamphlet, entitled "An inquiry into the obligation of Christians to use means for the conversion of the heathen." The effect of this pamphlet was marvellous, or rather the work itself was marvellous, and its effect only natural. It presented the duty of the Church so clearly that men dared no longer to disregard it ; and by this, the "young enthusiast" made his first real impression. In 1788 he removed from Moulton to Leicester, and became the pastor of the Baptist Church in Harvey Lane, afterward the scene of the labours of one of the most zealous supporters of the mission, the accom-

I

plished and eloquent Robert Hall. But his intense longing for the Gospel to be made known in distant lands was still undiminished.

Three years later, when he again introduced the question at a meeting of Baptist ministers, to his great delight he was encouraged by Mr. Sutcliffe and Mr. Andrew Fuller, each of whom preached a sermon in defence of him and in support of his proposal. Whilst opposition and discouragement had failed to quench the fire of his passion, sympathy served to fan it into a still fiercer flame, and at the next meeting of the Association, held at Nottingham in the spring of 1792, he preached a sermon on the subject. He chose for his text the words of Isaiah : "*Enlarge the place of thy tent, and let them stretch forth the curtains of thine habitations. Spare not; lengthen thy cords and strengthen thy stakes, for thou shalt break forth, on the right hand and on the left, and thy seed shall inherit the Gentiles, and make the desolate cities to be inhabited.*" The sermon, divided into two parts, "*Expect great things from God*" and "*attempt great things for God,*" was animating as it was criminating. Many who had openly opposed the project wept for shame ; others, who had treated it with indifference, were scarcely less affected ; old prejudices fell away, and it was at once resolved "that against the next ministers' meeting at Kettering, a plan should be prepared for the purpose of forming a Society for propagating the Gospel among the heathen." In accordance with this resolution, on Tuesday the 2nd of October, 1792, twelve men met together in a house at Kettering, by whom a Society was formed, to be called "The Particular Baptist Society for Propagating the Gospel among the Heathen."

This having been done, money was required ; and how much do you think was realised ? How many thousands of pounds do you suppose were laid upon God's altar, for the purpose of making known His love to the heathen world ? Talk not of thousands ! The whole fund with which this Society commenced operations amounted to £13 12s. 6d. The objectors to the scheme (for there were some who had survived the shocks of Carey's pamphlet and sermon), were amused. "What," said they, "is £13 the mighty sum with which it is proposed to undertake so vast a scheme?" Yes; it was contributed by a few earnest men, who gave what they could, and was as the first droppings of a series of showers of the most splendid generosity which the Christian world has ever known.

Six weeks later, Mr. Thomas, formerly a surgeon in Bengal, was accepted as the first Baptist missionary, and was directed to India. Carey was asked if he would accompany him, and scarcely was the question asked, when it was answered by a joyful "Yes," for though he had a desire to make his way to the South Sea Islands, he cared but little where he went so long as he could only have the opportunity of preaching the Gospel to those who had never heard it.

The Church at Harvey Lane at once gave up its pastor, and so far all was well, but unfortunately Mrs. Carey, forgetting the vow which she had made "to obey" her lord, absolutely and obstinately refused to accompany him. Doubtless this good man loved his wife much, but he loved his duty a great deal more, and therefore he resolved to go without her, and to take with him Felix, his eldest son.

A farewell service having been held at Leicester, the missionaries embarked for India. They were not yet, however, fairly off —the captain of the vessel having received an anonymous letter, warning him at his peril to proceed with them, at once ordered them to disembark. Poor Carey, stout-hearted as he was, was utterly dejected, whilst the no less indomitable Fuller exclaimed, "*We are all undone!*" It is often the case, however, that good is brought out of evil, and on this occasion (perhaps the only one since the creation of the world) good came out of an anonymous letter, for Mr. Thomas, doubtless prompted by pity for his lonely companion, visited Mrs. Carey, and prevailed upon her to accompany them, when it should be found possible for them to set sail ; and on the 13th day of April, 1793, they all embarked on board the *Kron Princess Maria.*

It was with a true, unselfish gladness that they broke away from their native land. They looked *forward* to the strange country, rather than *backward* upon old England ; and on the morning of the day on which they sailed, their joyous feelings were well expressed by one of them who wrote :—*" The ship is come, the signal made, the guns are fired, and we are going with a fine fair wind. Farewell ! my dear brethren and sisters, farewell ! May the God of Jacob be ours and yours, by sea and by land, for time and for eternity : most affectionately adieu !"*

No sooner had they bidden farewell to their friends in England, than Messrs. Carey and Thomas set to work at the translation of the Book of Genesis into Bengalee, a language familiar to one, and not altogether unknown by the other ; and on Nov. 7th they reached their much longed-for haven.

Such was the origin of the *Baptist Missionary Society;* for nearly ninety years it has existed, extending its operations year by year ; and to-day it matters not to which part of the globe we look, whether North or South, East or West, for in Europe, Asia, Africa, and America, there are God-fearing, Christ-loving men and women supported by this Society, the origin of whose work may be traced to the vigorous mind and the noble heart of William Carey.

On the arrival of the missionaries in India, they made their way to Calcutta, where, though kindly received by the natives, they remained only until they had arranged their secular affairs, and travelled about, viewing a small portion of the land which they had determined should be conquered for Christ. Right patiently and ploddingly did they labour, though they could see almost no results from their work. Being in a strange land, they were often sorely pressed by temporal needs. Heavy was the burden of affliction which had to be borne by each of them, yet they pushed along, unable to despair because of the conviction that God had sent them, and that God was with them. For some years they "*went about* doing good," until in the last year of the century they found a settled home at Serampore.

At a committee meeting held in 1795, two young men, Jacob Grigg and James Rodway, were selected to go out to Africa, and they set sail on Nov. 2nd of that year. Their prospects of success were most encouraging, but the health of the one, and the prudence of the other, proving defective, the one returned to England, and the other, hid his face, in America. The collapse of this mission to Africa, though greatly disappointing to the Committee, did not in the smallest degree, either shake its faith or damp its zeal.

Almost the only objection to mission enterprise which has survived to the present time is based upon the spiritual needs of our own country. "Why," it is sometimes asked, "should all this money and all this energy be expended in the attempt to convert the heathen world, when there is so much need for Gospel light at home?" This objection ought by this time to be worn out, for it was one of the earliest, and how do you think it was answered nearly a hundred years ago? Why, the first Baptist *Foreign* Missionary Society was the first Baptist *Home* Missionary Society ; a sum of money was voted out of the general funds for the purpose of evangelising *England.* So it has been ever since, and so it must always be. Let the missionary spirit be active, and the home of the mission will reap a large benefit.

In 1796, John Fountain was welcomed to the soil of Hindustan, and was followed, three years later, by Ward, Brunsdon, Grant, and Marshman. The attention of Carey and Thomas had from the first been given to *the translation of the Scriptures into the native tongues.* In their cabins on board the Kron Princess Maria, they commenced this work ; under the burning sun of India they continued it ; most devoted was their diligence, and almost incredible was their progress. Within five years after their arrival, they had completed translations of the

Pentateuch, the Psalms, Isaiah, Jeremiah, part of Ezekiel, and the whole of the New Testament ; and it was resolved to send from England a supply of paper for the *printing* of the New Testament. Thomas was no less earnest in this matter than Carey, and the latter entered into the spirit of the words of the former, who said, " I would give a million pounds sterling—if I had it—to see a Bengalee Bible."

Early in the first year of the present century, Mr. Carey arrived at Serampore, and this Danish settlement became thenceforth the headquarters of the Mission. The Governor was favourably disposed to the work, and suitable premises were obtained. The press, which had been fixed at Mudnabutty, was removed to Serampore, and with the indefatigable Ward to superintend it, whilst the Word of God was being preached to the thousands, it was printed for the *millions* of India.

The death of Mr. Fountain at this time cast a deep shadow over the brightening prospects of the Mission. His too short career had been one full of noble deeds. A stone was erected to mark the place of his burial, upon which, according to his own request, were inscribed the words, " John Fountain, missionary to the Indies, aged 33, *a sinner, saved by grace.*"

Up to this date, although a continually increasing band of men and women had been working for fully seven years, not a single Hindoo had given evidence of conversion to the Chrisian faith, but at length the reward of patient waiting came. On December 29th, 1800, Dr. Carey baptised his son, Felix, and the first Hindoo convert, named Krishnoo. We will not speculate as to which was the happier moment to him, that in which he led into the water his first-born son, or that in which he pronounced the sacred name over the first Bengali convert. The ceremony was witnessed by many hundreds of people who poured anathemas on the convert and his family, but in the crowd there was one who shed tears of joy, and that was the good-hearted Governor of the settlement. Other natives quickly followed the example of Krishnoo, and Carey's second son followed the example of his elder brother.

The membership of the Church rapidly increased to the number of thirty-six, consisting of fourteen Europeans, and twenty-two natives. Preaching was commenced at Calcutta, and the printing press was kept steadily at work. The Pentateuch, the Psalms, the Prophecies of Isaiah, and the New Testament, had already been printed, and it was the ambition and the intention of the missionaries to circulate the Word of God in *ten* distinct languages.

Early in 1805 an insurrection broke out at Vellore, in which a number of British soldiers were massacred, for which these simple-hearted peace-loving men were blamed ; and though it was proved that not a single missionary had approached that part of Hindustan, certain reports being carried over to England, an attempt was made to work upon the fears of the Government, and induce the authorities to recall the missionaries. For this purpose, pamphlets were published by individual writers, which were full of invective, whilst the *Edinburgh Reviewers* joined in the attack, and directed their bitterest sarcasm against Carey and his fellow-workers. Mr. Andrew Fuller, who was the very soul of the Mission, at once joined issue with these assailants ; pamphlet followed pamphlet in quick succession, each of which was a masterly production of his splendid mind. The *Quarterly Review* also took up the question, and boldly defended the missionaries. Replying to their opponents, who called them *fools, madmen, Tinkers, Calvinists, and schismatics,* the *Quarterly Review* says : " *These low-born and low-bred mechanics have translated the whole Bible into Bengalee, and have by this time printed it. They are printing the New Testament in the Sanscrit, the Orissa, Maharatta, Hindustanee, and Guzarat, and translating it into Persic, Feluiga, Karnata, Chinese, and the language of the Seiks and of the Burmans; and in four of these languages they are going on with the Bible. Extraordinary as this is, it will appear more so when it is remembered, that of these men, one was originally a shoemaker, another a printer at Hull, and a third, the master of a charity school at Bristol. Only fourteen years have elapsed since Thomas and Carey set foot in India, and in that time have these misssonaries acquired this gift of tongues. In fourteen years these low-born and low-bred mechanics have done more towards spreading the knowledge of the Scriptures among the heathen, than has been accomplished, or even attempted, by all the world besides."*

These opponents having been vanquished, the work progressed more rapidly than formerly. In 1807, operations were commenced in Burmah, and two years later there were, in all, nine stations occupied by ten Europeans and two native missionaries ; and in 1811, the number of members in all the stations exceeded three hundred, one-third of whom had been received into fellowship in a little more than a year.

On March 11th, 1811, fire broke out in the printing office at Serampore, and the building, 200 feet long, was totally destroyed. Paper, type, manuscripts, and books were also consumed ; and the total loss amounted to the value of £10,000. As soon as the intelligence of this disaster arrived in England, the Christian people of all denominations became eager to repair the loss. A subscription list was opened, and now we may talk of thousands, for one thousand pounds followed another thousand pounds, until, in a little more than six weeks after the news of the fire was known, Mr. Fuller suggested, that as the entire amount had been collected, *they were bound in all honesty to stop the contributions.*

Undoubted progress was now made. The hearts of the natives seemed gradually opened for the reception of the Word ; and to the joy of all, and to the unspeakable rapture of one, another of Dr. Carey's sons became decided for Christ and dedicated to his service. Jabez Carey had displayed a most decided aversion to Christianity. At the first annual meeting of the Society held in London, Dr. Ryland referred to the happiness of Dr. Carey in having two of his sons working with him, " but," he said, " there is a third who gives him pain. *Brethren, let us send up a united, universal, and fervent prayer to God, for the conversion of Jabez Carey.*" A most solemn and prayerful spirit at once fell upon the audience ; and—call it a coincidence if you will—amongst the first letters afterward received from India, was the announcement of that conversion, which was said to have taken place almost at the very hour of prayer in London. Jabez Carey was cordially accepted as a member of the missionary staff ; and his father and two brothers united in "laying hands" upon him.

In the year 1813, considerable interest was awakened by the question of renewing the Charter of the East India Company. It was no secret that this Company was most unfriendly to the work of the missionaries, who were compelled to proceed to India by the circuitous route of America. Andrew Fuller and Robert Hall united in a vigorous and successful effort to secure the insertion of a clause in the renewed Charter, "authorising the peaceful dissemination of the gospel in India." Four clauses were inserted, favourable to "persons desirous of going to India for the purpose of promoting the religious and moral improvement of the natives."

In the following year a heavy loss was sustained in the death of Mr. Sutcliffe, who had from the first been a staunch friend to the Mission. Born in Halifax in the year 1752, after spending a life distinguished for prudence, kindness, and integrity, he died on the 22nd of June, 1814, in the 62nd year of his age.

Mr. Sutcliffe had been for many years the intimate friend of Mr. Andrew Fuller, and they were scarcely divided even in death, for within twelve months of the decease of the one, Mr. Fuller, who had been secretary of the Society ever since its formation, was also called away. The extraordinary power of this popular preacher is well known. He proved himself to be, if not a ready, at least a dangerous foe in controversy. He was eminently adapted *to lead men.* He spent a life of splendid industry, and having "served his generation, fell on sleep."

During the years 1815-16-17, upwards of 400 members were
added to the chapels in India, and in the last of these years, the
total membership was not less than 1,200. Day and Sunday
schools were conducted at almost every station; and the translation
of the Scriptures already completed, together with that in process
of being carried out, gave the Word of God, in its own language,
to almost every nation from China to the borders of Persia, *comprising nearly a half of the entire human race.*

But before we leave this, the FIRST PERIOD of Missions, we
must refer to the formation of our own Society.

In 1809, the Rev. J. G. Pike, of Derby, author of "Persuasives
to Early Piety," and similar works, at the annual Association
of the *General* Baptist Churches, held at Quorndon, in the county
of Leicester, suggested, overtures having been made in vain to
co-operate with the existing *Particular* Baptist Society, that they
themselves should engage a missionary, and form an additional Society
for propagating the Gospel among the heathen. His suggestion
was not then carried into effect, but his appeals were in-
cessant and his enthusiasm contagious, and the fire at Serampore
co-operating to awaken sympathy in the hearts of all Christians,
a resolution was passed at the Association held at Boston in June,
1816, that "a GENERAL BAPTIST MISSIONARY SOCIETY should
be established." The first missionaries of this Society, Messrs.
Bampton and Peggs, set sail in May of 1821, and reached Serampore in the following November. They proceeded to the province
of Orissa, in which well chosen field they have been succeeded by
an illustrious band of devoted men and women.*

And now, having glanced at the principal features of Indian
Missions during the first quarter of a century of its existence, let
us turn to what may be called the SECOND PERIOD of the Mission's
history, the most prominent feature of which is the unparalleled
progress of the work in Jamaica.

For some time the Gospel had been preached on this island
by certain freed men from America; and at length Mr. John Rowe

was sent out by the Society ; others followed him, but the climate being unfavourable to the health of Europeans, some were removed by death, and sickness compelled others to withdraw. With the arrival of Mr. and Mrs. Coultart, the JAMAICA Mission may be said to have been fairly commenced in the year 1817, the 25th year after the formation of the Particular Baptist Society.

On the arrival of Mr. and Mrs. Coultart, they applied themselves with much heartiness to their duties amongst the simple-minded Negroes. In 1822, only five years after their landing, Mr. Thomas Knibb arrived and found a Church of 2,700 members ; on the second Sunday which he spent on the island he baptised 152 converts ; but the work of Thomas Knibb was speedily brought to a close by his deeply lamented death, the vacancy caused by which was promptly filled by his more illustrious brother *William*, whose name is still familiar to the freedom-loving people of the whole world.

Fourteen years after the arrival of Mr. and Mrs. Coultart, there were on the island twenty-four churches, presided over by fourteen missionaries. During the year 1830 nearly 2,000 had been baptised, making a total membership of the Baptist Churches in Jamaica, 10,838. It is impossible to say where this rapid growth would have stopped, had it not been checked by an event apparently most terrible, yet in reality most glorious.

Towards the close of '31, a report was circulated amongst the slaves that a *"free paper"* had arrived from England, which gave to them a right to liberty. The missionaries assured them that they had been deceived, but so eagerly did they long for freedom, that the great mass of them resolved that they would not work for their masters after Christmas. When the insurrection broke out, the missionaries were accused of having incited the slaves to rebellion. Abbot, Knibb, Gardner, and Burchell were arrested on this charge, the animosity shewn towards them by the white people being most fierce. As Mr. Burchell was being conducted through the streets, they thronged round him in a frenzy of excitement, gnashing their teeth in rage, and shouting, "Hang him!" "Shoot him!" "Have his blood!" and had it not been for the protection afforded by the *coloured* people, who had learned to love these men, he would doubtless have been murdered. "*Yea*," to use his own words, "*I should have been torn limb from limb by my countrymen, yea, by enlightened, respectable Christian Britons.*"

The assizes were opened and the missionaries tried. Numbers of witnesses had been bribed to give evidence against them, but the Negroes were too simple for their cowardly masters; so amusingly false were their statements, that it was utterly impossible to convict, and consequently, to the grievous disappointment of judge and jury, they were discharged, without one of their own witnesses being called, 300 of whom had voluntarily come together from all parts of the island. Mobs were thereupon organised for the purpose of destroying the Baptist chapels, and the *Colonial Church Union having pledged itself to support and protect the chapel destroyers*, they were made bold to do their work most completely. Almost every chapel and other building belonging to the Mission was either totally destroyed or seriously damaged, the total loss thus caused amounting to more than £23,000.

When quietness had been partially restored, Messrs. Knibb and Burchell came over to England, that they might represent the true state of affairs, and they found much practical sympathy with the Christian public. Upon the details of their visit I have no right to dwell. They went to the root of the matter, and demanded the abolition of slavery. We know what a victory they won. The effect of Mr. Knibb's speeches was most striking; those who listened to him, and those who read his words, were aroused to a state of wildest excitement. Not only the Baptist denomination, but all Christian people were stirred to their very souls. Public opinion rolled on as a resistless torrent; it could not be stopped, it could not be checked; with ever increasing

volume it rushed on, and *the fate of slavery was sealed.*
Whenever we are reminded of the emancipation of the slaves,
let us not fail to think of the names of William Knibb, Thomas
Burchell, and their co-workers, not only Baptists, but Baptist
missionaries, to whose impassioned exertions it was most largely
due.

The appeals for money to repair the damage done to the
Mission property were readily responded to. A grant of more
than £11,000 was made by Government, to which the sum of
£14,000 was added by the British public. In the meantime, the
members of the churches in Jamaica clung to their principles and
to their pastors with most commendable tenacity. The congregations rapidly increased. Multitudes flocked into the Church,
and the school became more prosperous than ever.

In the autumn of '34, Messrs. Knibb and Burchell returned,
and the reception given by the natives is described as being most
enthusiastic. They looked at them all round, scarcely believing
their own senses ; they laughed, and they wept, but both for joy ;
they clapped their hands and waved their hats, " and when the
whole multitude, consisting of three or four thousand, set up
their shouts, they made the whole town resound with their
thundering huzzas."

In 1833, the Mission was extended to the Bahamas. Already
about twenty churches had been established in these islands, but
the people were in a most benighted condition, and Mr. Burton
states, that the first prayer he heard, offered by one of the members
of one of the most influential churches in the Colony, was partly
offered to Abraham, Isaac, and Jacob.

Turning our attention again to the work carried on in India,
the progress which was made, though not so evident, was probably
not less real than that in Jamaica. Many new institutions were
established. The native mind became more and more willing to
receive the truths of the Gospel, and converts were being
continually received into the Church.

In 1818, Serampore College was founded, and the usefulness of the " Benevolent Institution,' a school established some years previously in Calcutta, began to be observed.   The Mission press was kept working with unflagging rapidity.   Sutteeism was abolished, very largely through the determined efforts of the missionaries. The connection of the Government with Juggernaut was greatly weakened by them ; whilst caste had received at their hands a shock from which it has never recovered.   In the month of March, 1840, " The Bible Translation Society " was established, and the invaluable services which it has ever since rendered to the Mission gives it a claim upon all English Baptists.

Whilst referring to this stage of the Missions' history, we must not fail to make mention of the death of its great originator, Dr. William Carey.   On the 9th of June, 1834, he passed away to his great reward.   He was a splendid specimen of what a man may become by the grace of God.   Eminently simple in his manner ; full of benevolence ; whole-hearted in everything which he undertook ; carried along by a mighty, Christlike love for his fellow men, he had worked most devotedly through a life of more than three-score years and ten ; and the epitaph chosen for himself by this distinguished scholar, skilful teacher, and unselfish philanthropist was simply this :—

"A guilty, weak, and helpless worm,
    On thy kind arms I fall ;
    Be thou my strength and righteousness,
    My Saviour and my all."

In 1837, Mr. Pearce, one of the missionaries in India, visited England, when he was successful in creating a more lively interest in the Eastern Mission.   He begged that ten more men might be sent out to India, and that £6,000 might be contributed to aid them in their work.   He said, "When I asked a number of children what I should bring them from Europe, even they asked for more missionaries to instruct themselves and their country men." His appeals were so earnestly made, and the necessity for providing

all that he requested was made so apparent, that both men and
money were speedily forthcoming.

During this quarter of a century, new stations were opened
in India and Ceylon ; and in addition to the Bahamas, Central
America received the missionaries, whilst assistance was also
rendered to the Church of Christ in South Africa.

At the close of this period, fifty years after the first meeting
of the Society was held at Kettering, the churches of the East
Indies were composed of 978 members, with about 300 Europeans
in separate fellowship. The number of members in Jamaica was
32,000 ; in the Bahamas, 1,176 ; and in Central America, 132.
Native helpers had sprung up to strengthen the hands, and lighten
the burdens of the European missionaries, and the number of
children receiving secular and religious instruction was, in the
West 6,700, and in the East 2,700.

In the year 1842, the Jubilee services were held at Kettering.
Only one of the founders of the Mission survived to this date,
the Venerable Reynold Hogg, who at the age of *ninety* years
joined, with all youthfulness of soul, in the jubilant song of
praise which was sung, and in the sanguine predictions of future
progress. During the Jubilee year, £33,000 were raised, by which
a heavy debt was removed, premises in Moorgate Street erected,
and new missions started in Trinidad and Hayti.

As we look westwards at this period, we discover that the
emancipation of the slaves had produced a most remarkable effect
upon the natives of Jamaica. Crime was almost unknown on the
island, save when committed by the white people. At the Assizes
held in a district of 125,000 inhabitants, nineteen were tried, six
of whom were white men, and three of the natives were acquitted.
At the Quarter Sessions held in a parish of 30,000 inhabitants,
only one person was tried ; and when Mr. Gurney visited the gaol
at Falmouth, he found there only one person, and that one was a
white man. Mr. Knibb paid a visit to one of the largest gaols on
the island, and seeing the treadmill, asked permission to go on it,

but the supervisor said, "Mr. Knibb, it's no use, it is rusty, for since *the first of August,* we have never been able to muster hands enough to turn it." In the parish of St. Ann's, where Mr. Abbot laboured, the gaol had been closed for six months, and the gaoler pensioned off until he should be wanted again.

The membership of the churches increased most rapidly, many of the scenes described by the historian reminding one of the day of Pentecost. So strong indeed did the cause become, that at a united meeting of the missionaries, it was unanimously resolved to detach themselves from the funds of the parent Society, and trust, for their entire support, to the liberality of their own churches.

Immediately after the liberation of the slaves, the Negro members of the Jamaica churches were fired by the noble ambition to carry the Gospel into their fatherland. A black man named Keith sold all that he possessed, and worked his way out to Africa, with the intention of preaching Christ on the very spot where he had been stolen. He was not disappointed, for he did stand upon that spot, and in his own simple manner besought his fellow countrymen to embrace the religion of Christ. Many others were actuated by the same spirit of unselfish love. Mr. Knibb, having called together twenty or thirty of the African members of the churches at Kingston, informed them of his intention to visit Africa, at once they expressed a desire to accompany him. One of them said, "I will go with you as your shoeblack, if you will take me." He asked him when he would be ready to go. "To-morrow," was the prompt reply. "But," said Mr. Knibb, "perhaps you would be made slaves again, if you went into Africa." And what do you think was the answer given by these men who were only just released from cruel bondage? They replied, "*We have been made slaves for men, we can be made slaves for Christ.*" The Committee cheerfully took up this work, and commenced a Mission to Western Africa. The Rev. J. Clarke and Dr. Prince were sent out from England, and selected, as the seat of the Mission, the Island of Fernando Po ; there they formed a Church, and were shortly afterwards joined by four additional missionaries and eight teachers. But the Spanish Government, to which the island belonged, having previously sent Jesuit priests to instruct the people, in the year 1858, proclaimed the religion of the Colony to be that of the Roman Catholic Church, though there was not a single native Roman Catholic on the island. All other forms of religion were prohibited ; and the result was, that not a few, preferring religious liberty in a strange land to a fettered conscience at home, went out to the foot of the mountain of Cameroons, where the Colony of Victoria was established, and where they were permitted to worship God in their own way.

In 1843, a Mission which had for some time been worked by the Welsh churches, in Brittany, was taken over by the Society. The Scriptures were printed in the Breton language, and there, in spite of the hostility of the priests, chapels were erected and the Gospel very successfully preached.

It had long been desired that something should be done for the salvation of the millions in China, but it appeared impossible to establish a Mission there until the year 1859. The Rev. John Angell James, believing that the right time had then come, called the churches to the enterprise, and two men, both of them acquainted with the language, were despatched to the port of Chefoo, where, in the face of the most bitter opposition, they established a Baptist Church.

In the year 1850, the Mission in India was visited in behalf of the Society by the Revs. J. Russell and Dr. Leechman. They spent about twelve months in examining the stations in Ceylon, Madras, Bengal, and the North West Provinces of India. The report which they presented on their return was highly gratifying ; they were fully convinced of the reality of the conversions which had been recorded ; whilst the general condition of the churches, the success of the College at Serampore, and the

K

eminent usefulness of the Mission press, gave to them the most complete satisfaction.

The year 1857 was doubtless, in many respects, the most memorable in the history of Indian Missions. At this period, events occurred which threatened to involve not only the Christian Church which had been established there, but also our Eastern Empire itself, in utter ruin. We refer to the *Indian mutiny.* For many months the labours of the missionaries were entirely suspended. All they could do was to look on whilst the most horrible atrocities were committed, to keep out of the way of danger as far as possible, and to hide themselves from the ferocity of those who thirsted for English blood. One, and strange to say, one only of the Baptist missionaries fell a prey to this deadly animosity. This was J. Mackay, who had displayed the utmost zeal in the Mission work. Of the native Christians, many suffered the most terrible persecutions, and not a few, after being tortured to the extemity of human endurance, died as Christian witnesses should die, courageously, and even cheerfully, being sustained by the assurance that they laid down their lives in the service of their crucified Lord.

In looking at this quarter of a century, 1843-67, we find that 100 new missionaries had been sent out from England, making a total of 229 since the formation of the Society, and the services of 300 native evangelists were engaged. There were at the close of this period, stations in India, Ceylon, China, Western Africa, Jamaica, Hayti, Trinidad, The Bahama Islands, Brittany, and Norway. There had been an increase in the membership of almost all the churches. In India, the membership had risen during the twenty-five years from 1,278 to 2,300 ; showing a gain of more than 1,000, allowing for all deductions. Excluding Jamaica, the period commenced with 1,580 members in the West, and closed with 3,200. In Jamaica the membership decreased, but this is fully accounted for by the ravages of cholera and small-pox, which in the year 1850 threatened to depopulate the island,

and which cut off about ten per cent. of the native Christians. A considerable number were received into fellowship, and notwithstanding very large deductions, in the year 1867 the churches in Jamaica' contained from 20,000 to 25,000 members.

The translation of the Scriptures was carried on in the East with unabated zeal. The schools both in the East and West were largely multiplied. The day scholars connected with all the schools, excepting those in Jamaica, numbered not less than 3,000 ; and in Jamaica there were 2,451 day, and more than 10,000 Sunday scholars.

Having now arrived at the year 1867, we will simply refer to the statements contained in the report presented in March of last year to show the progress during the past few years.

In China there are three missionaries, nineteen chapels, and 500 Church members. On the Island of Ceylon, four missionaries report that they have twenty-nine stations, twenty chapels, thirty-three school houses, and a total of 670 members.

In India there are thirty-five missionaries, 110 stations; ninety chapels, and a membership of 3,796.

In the West Indies and Africa, excluding Jamaica, there are fifteen missionaries, forty-eight stations, ninety-seven chapels, and 5,238 church members ; whilst in Jamaica there are six missionaries, partly or totally supported by the Society, fifty-one pastors of self-supporting Baptist churches, 123 stations, and 22,767 members.

There is also an evangelical Mission in Rome. James Wall was among the first to enter the city on the destruction of the Pope's temporal power; and at the present time, three of the Society's missionaries are in Rome, who are assisted by eight evangelists, and report a membership of 133.

Taking a summary of the statistics for the year ending March 31st, 1880, we have the following interesting figures. There are sixty-eight missionaries wholly supported, and fourteen partly supported by the funds of the Society, and 57 pastors of self-supporting churches.   There are 241 evangelists, 407 stations, and 33,805 church members.

The labours of the General Baptist missionaries have been similar to those of their brethren and sisters of the Particular Baptist Missionary Society. They, like them, have been diligent in translating and printing the Scriptures, providing school books and general literature, and careful to educate the Hindoo youth. They have held to their posts in the face of difficulty, persecution, and death ; and they too have been rewarded by large conquests over heathen superstition.   The fires of *suttee* have been extinguished ; *infanticide* has been abolished ; *human sacrifices* have been abandoned, and "victims rescued from a barbarous death have presented themselves a living sacrifice to God ; " "the *Churruck Poojah*, or swinging on hooks, has been suppressed ; " orphanages have been established, and numbers were rescued from the cruel horrors of the terrible Orissa famine, Churches and Christian villages have been established, and a glorious work done for God and souls. The names of Lacey, Sutton, Goadby, Buckley, Bailey, Miller, Brooks, Packer, Stubbins, Wilkinson, and many others not less worthy of mention, remind us of strong faith, heroic effort, Christ-like zeal, and continuous success in the evangelisation of Orissa.   The report of 1880 shows that sixteen missionaries, male and female, are supported in their work amongst the millions of Orissa, by twenty native preachers.   The number of chapels is twelve, and the total membership, 994.   Besides that, we have a Mission in Rome, under the superintendence of the Rev. N. H. Shaw, assisted by Paul Grassi, once a Canon of the Romish Church.

It is characteristic of all kinds of Christian work that its results can never be fully shown by statistics ; and this is particularly the case in regard to the Mission enterprise.   It is not a little thing to know that so many thousands have been won from their idolatry and superstition to the service of the true God ; but if not one single conversion had been brought about, the work of Carey and his successors would have been by no means in vain. If nothing else had been done, the regions of idolatry have been penetrated, and at least an opening made for the Gospel by the *breaking of caste.* Not only has a victory been gained over caste, but a scarcely less illustrious triumph has been won over language, and the native tongues of the millions of heathendom have been made to communicate the truths of Christ's Gospel. Churches have been established in every quarter of the globe, which have themselves become centres of usefulness ; whilst, not least, a generous missionary spirit has been created and sustained for nearly a hundred years in the hearts of Christian English people. Many memorable days have there been in the history of Christianity, and in the history of India during the last hundred years, but, few more memorable than the 2nd day of October, 1792. *The character of the Indian Empire has been changed by the unselfish charity of the English Baptists*, and many are the millions who have, directly or indirectly, been blessed by their labours.

Our duty is to *pray*, to *give*, and to *believe.* Let not that strong missionary spirit which has been displayed for nearly a century be suffered to languish now. Christ died for the inhabitants of India, and of China, and of Africa, as well as for the people of England, and the blessings of His Gospel are suited equally to men of all climes and of all characters. May the work of Christian missionaries prosper, and may the time come quickly when that divinely taught prayer, which has been breathed by the Church every day for eighteen hundred years, shall be answered, and God's kingdom come, and His "will be done in earth as it is in heaven.'"

THE BAPTISTS & THE ABOLITION OF SLAVERY,

REV. GEORGE WILSON M'CREE.

SLAVERY is an ancient curse. It has afflicted and degraded humanity from the earliest ages. The Chaldeans held men in slavery. The youths of Lacedemonia slew, for amusement, three hundred slaves in one night. In the year 337 B.C. Attica contained four hundred thousand bondmen and bondwomen. The Romans chained slaves to their gates to act as porters to their guests. Our own Alfred the Great made laws respecting slaves on English soil, which was to be often wet with their tears and blood. In Bristol market, children were sold like cattle for exportation. Queen Elizabeth had slaves, whose freedom, however, she promoted. And, in fact, slavery prevailed in England in some form or other, until the year 1772, when, it was decided in our Courts of Law, that slavery could not exist within the blue seas that wash our shores, and that any slave landing on British ground became free.

The prevalence of slavery in the world so late as 1840 may be seen in the vital statistics of that time. In the United States, the slave population was 2,750,000; in the Brazils, 2,500,000; in the Spanish colonies, 600,000; in the French colonies, 265,000; in the Dutch colonies, 70,000; and an innumerable multitude was held in bondage by Oriental powers and people.

In reference to the United States, it may be noted here, that at the World's Anti-Slavery Convention assembled in London in

May, 1840, a letter, signed David Marks, was read from the Free-Will Baptists, which contained this memorable declaration:—"As a people we mourn that the Church in this land is so deeply involved in the sin of slavery, and have endeavoured to keep our garments pure and unspotted from its foul stains. We neither receive into our churches, or at the communion table, *any* whose hands are polluted with slavery. Our Board of Foreign Missions refuse to receive any donations or bequests from slaveholders, on the principle that their wealth is the wages of iniquity and the price of blood." Such a noble declaration deserves immortal record, and shows that there were Baptists then who had long been in the van of Human Progress, and were splendid examples of enlightened manhood.

We may well marvel that so late as 1772 slaves were permitted to remain bondmen in England. A brighter era then dawned. James Somerset was an African slave, the property of Mr. Charles Stewart, and was brought to London by his master in 1769. Finding himself in England, he claimed the right to belong to himself, and left his master, who, thereupon, had him seized, and sent on board the *Ann and Mary* to be deported to the West Indies as a slave. His case was brought before the Judges by Mr. Granville Sharp, and, after the case had been argued at three different sittings, it was proclaimed, "That as soon as ever any slave set his foot upon English territory he became free." This memorable verdict from the Bench inspired William Cowper to pen these noble words :—

> " Slaves cannot breathe in England, if their lungs
> Receive our air, that moment they are free :
> They touch our country, and their shackles fall.
> That's noble, and bespeaks a nation proud
> And jealous of the blessing. Spread it, then,
> And let it circulate through every vein
> Of all your Empire; that, where Britain's power
> Is felt, mankind may feel her mercy too."

But this decision of the Judges did not abolish the African Slave Trade. Three centuries ago the Spaniards commenced that atrocious traffic. Tens of thousands of African men, women, and children were torn from their homes; were chained, beaten, insulted, outraged, and sold like cattle at the coast, and taken in slave-ships (where hundreds of them died, in the small holds, of suffocation, and were then thrown to the sharks), to the West Indies, and there consigned to hopeless bondage.

It took William Wilberforce, Thomas Clarkson, and other great Englishmen, twenty years of laborious agitation to induce the British Parliament to abolish the Slave Trade; but, at last, the glorious victory was won, and, on Wednesday, the 25th of March, 1807, to use the words of Thomas Clarkson, "as the sun was in its meridian splendour to witness this august act, the establishment of a Magna Charta for Africa in Great Britain was completed."

The abolition of the Slave Trade did not, however, sweep the curse of Slavery from the West Indies. It still flourished in deadly luxuriance there. Commenced by the Spaniards, who had destroyed the aborigines of Jamaica, it was continued by the English, and for two hundred and fifty years the slave-ship bore its living cargo to the shores of that beautiful island, "where only man was vile."

On these enslaved sons and daughters of Africa the pure light of the Gospel dawned through one of their own race. His name was George Lisle. He was a freed negro from Virginia, a member of a Baptist Church, and when he came to Jamaica, and arrived in Kingston, he began to preach the Gospel to them. In a room he formed a church of four members—all of them refugees from the United States. Working diligently with his hands, he went on preaching, and in seven years he baptized five hundred persons, and presided over a church of three hundred and fifty members. He had incredible annoyances. A gentleman rode his horse into the chapel, and cried, "Now, old Lisle, give my horse the Sacrament !" Mr. Lisle replied, with quiet dignity, "No, Sir, you are not fit yourself to receive it." His enemies cast him into prison, loaded him with irons, tried him for his life, but had at last to set him free.

Moses Baker was another pioneer of Gospel freedom. He was once a drunken negro, but he and his wife having been converted to God and baptized, joined the church of which Mr. Lisle was the pastor, Moses Baker became a preacher, and had access to twenty sugar estates. God greatly blessed him to the degraded negroes, but, one Sunday, a planter's book-keeper heard him give out the words of a hymn :—

> "Shall we go on in sin,
>   Because Thy grace abounds,
>   Or crucify the Lord again,
>   And open all His wounds ?
>
> * * *
>
> "We will be slaves no more,
>   Since Christ has made us free,
>   He's nailed our tyrants to the Cross,
>   And bought our liberty."

And he charged the innocent evangelist with teaching the slaves rebellion and sedition. He was arrested, put in irons, and brought down to Montego Bay, where he was admitted to bail. As nothing disloyal could be proved against him, he was released, and went forth as before on his holy mission.

A great era now begins to dawn upon the West Indies. The roseate morning of the day of Freedom was at hand. In January, 1821, Messrs. Phillippo, Phillips, and Burchell arrived in Jamaica. Chiefly, at present, we shall speak of Thomas Burchell. A cultivated man, of fine presence, gentle, but fearless, saintly in spirit, an eloquent preacher, and a true man in all things, he was destined to play a leading part in the battle of emancipation. In February, 1825, William Knibb, surnamed the Lion-Hearted, followed, and Jamaica's soil was now trod by two of the noblest men the modern church ever had. "There were giants in those days."

Thomas Burchell's ministry was soon made useful to hundreds of coloured persons, mostly slaves. In June, 1827, there were eight Baptist churches in the island, comprising 5,246 members. Conflicts and persecutions were common. The missionaries were hated by the planters and the mob, and they were often slandered, insulted, and cast into prison. Two men, members of Mr. Burchell's church, had their houses levelled, their feet put into the stocks, and were sent in chains to the workhouse, simply for praying to their God ! One of them prayed so much in his chains, however, that he was told to go, and he went forthwith.

James Finlayson was a coloured man, who proceeded to market one Sunday to sell his honey. Wandering into Mr. Mann's chapel, he heard the Gospel, became anxious about his salvation, left his honey to take care of itself, and went away home. Having believed in Christ, he was baptized by Mr. Burnley, and, being a zealous man, he began to tell his brother slaves "what a dear Saviour he had found." For this he was flogged nearly to death. Such atrocious cruelty was often inflicted upon devout slaves who were members of churches, and they had no redress whatever. Nevertheless, the Word of God prevailed, and in 1831 the clear increase of the Baptist Churches was about 2,000, making a total of 10,838 members.

Now began a great and weary fight for Freedom. Englishmen were free, but they maintained slavery abroad, and felt and spoke like certain Americans in our time :—

> " I do believe in Freedom's cause,
>   As far away as Paris is ;
> I love to see her stick her claws
>   In them infernal Pharisees.
> It's very well agin a king
>   To draw resolves and triggers,
> But Liberty's a kind of thing
>   That don't agree with niggers."

But the bondmen of Jamaica would not wait on the pleasure of planters and Britons. They struck a heavy blow for their freedom. A terrible insurrection broke out in 1832—a fiery volcano of passion and murder. Fire, destruction, struggle, and death raged like a tornado. The planters were like madmen thirsting for blood. They shot the negroes as though they were dogs. Scores of slaves hung dead from trees on every roadside. Messrs. Knibb, Whitehorn, and Abbot were made prisoners, put into a canoe, taken for seven hours under a burning sun to Montego Bay, and finally consigned to a prison, the mob swearing their blood should redden the stones in the morning.

The personal narrative of William Knibb of this episode in his history is full of interest. He says :

"On Monday, the 2nd of January, after committing ourselves and our little ones to the divine protection, I went to the Court-house, and was forced to enlist, or to be enrolled, in the 4th company as a private soldier, but was granted leave of absence until the following morning, on account of indisposition.

"Tuesday, 3rd. Not knowing what might befall me this day, I took a solemn farewell of my dear wife and children, earnestly commending them to the care of that God who had hitherto never failed to be our help. With calm reliance upon my Heavenly Father, I went to perform my duties as a soldier, though rather anxious, from the conviction that my life would be attempted by the infuriated whites whenever I left the town. Soon, however, God released me from one trouble by permitting another to overtake me. While exhorting one of my deacons, Lewis Williams, to live near to God, I was arrested in the most brutal manner by a man named Paul Doeg commanding two black men to take me prisoner, he paraded before me in all the pomp of petty power, with a drawn sword, and had me conveyed to the guard room. Soon afterwards I was removed to the barracks, where I found brethren Whitehouse and Abbott, who, like myself, were under arrest, none of us knowing why or wherefore. In about an hour

Captain Christie came and informed us that Colonel Cadien had
sent him to tell us that we were to be sent to headquarters at
Montego Bay, and that a conveyance would be ready in half-an-
hour. I asked permission to see my wife and children, but was
denied this pleasure. I then requested to write to them, but this
small gratification was refused. Soon afterwards we were searched.
When all was ready, we were paraded through the streets to the
sea-side, guarded by four soldiers with a sergeant, and put into an
open canoe. After a long and tedious voyage of seven hours, we
were landed at Montego Bay about seven in the evening. The
canoe being leaky, my feet were completely soaked, and this, as I
had taken medicine, tended to increase the indisposition under
which I was labouring. On landing we were marched to the
Court-house, then to head-quarters, Sir William Cotton's, back to
the Court-house, then up a steep hill to his honour the custos's,
then back to the Court-house (which was a barracks), where we
were placed in the jury-box under a guard of four soldiers,
militiamen. Every epithet of abuse that infuriated malice could
invent was heaped upon me. The most horrid oaths that men or
devils could conceive were poured upon us, with the most vulgar
allusions that depraved nature could imagine. Twice was a
bayonet pointed at my breast, and when I requested permission
to lie down on the floor, being ill and fatigued (having been
harassed since the morning) I was damned and blasted, and
told that if I moved I should be instantly shot. Hell could
scarcely be worse. Value your privileges, ye Britons, and feel
and pray for those poor Christian slaves who are entirely
under the control of such beings. No Algerine pirate, or savage
Moor, would have treated me worse than I was treated by
Englishmen.

" No fault had I committed ; with none was I charged ; but I
was a missionary, and that was enough. I was calm, and happy,
and thankful that I felt a disposition to pray for my enemies, who
were taunting me that I should be shot on the morrow, and

pleasing themselves with the sport. In the midst of this, and when all seemed against us, God raised up a friend in Mr. Roby, who, after much trouble and fatigue, succeeded in delivering us from our foes, and provided for us a bed in his own office. About twelve at night we had the pleasure of praying unmolested, of thanking God for his great kindness in not permitting us to be murdered, and of laying our weary limbs to rest.

"On Wednesday morning the same kind friend procured our liberation on bail—J. Manderson, Esq., Member of Assembly, standing bail for me. Our good wives had arrived by land, and again we joined in grateful thanksgiving to that God who was better to us than all our fears. The same day I was attacked with fever brought on by exposure, wet feet, and anxiety. God mercifully restored me, and enabled me to cast my cares upon Him."

The noble spirit of William Knibb is further seen in an affecting letter to his mother :—

"Montego Bay, Feb. 10, 1832.

" Whether this will be the last letter you will receive from your son, is known only to that kind and indulgent God who has hitherto preserved my unworthy life. To give you a detailed statement of the scenes through which I have lately passed is impossible ; my soul hath them in remembrance, and is humbled within me. What is before me I cannot tell, but all is known to that God whose I am, and whom I serve. O, for grace and faith to trust him ! Through the medium of Mr. Gotch you will, I expect, have heard that I was taken a prisoner on the charge of being concerned in the rebellion that has broken out among the slaves. Although I have been five weeks in this state, or rather on bail, I do not know yet what the specific charges are. I know that I am innocent ; but such is the awful state of feeling here, that my only hope of escape is in Him who turneth the hearts of men as the rivers of water are turned. Should I escape I shall return to England, as I am not safe from assassination in this part of the world. Our chapels at this place, at Falmouth, Rio Buene, and I doubt not at other places, are levelled with the ground. Two days ago I escaped for my life, and took refuge on board one of His Majesty's ships in the harbour. I have this morning returned, being bound not to leave this place. Does my mother ask me, Do you repent becoming a missionary? My answer is, NO ; gladly would I spend the few remaining days of my pilgrimage in this land, were it the will of God. That I should not be tried and found guilty appears at present to be impossible. May the Lord in his great mercy direct me to act as in his sight ! My dear Mary is divinely supported under this deep trial, and has been of much comfort to me. May the Lord in his tender mercy prepare her for every afflictive dispensation ! The two children, William and Catherine, I have not seen for five weeks. I believe they are well ; may the Lord protect and preserve them. Little Ann is with us in ill health. I have been informed this morning that the mob have destroyed, or intended to destroy, my books and furniture. I shall feel the loss of the books much, as I have striven hard for seven years to obtain them, and intended them as a legacy to my children ; however, may God grant a sanctified use, and all will be well. The kindness of my thrice dear people at Falmouth makes my heart over-flow with gratitude to God ; my heart is with them, but I fear I shall never preach to them again. Of the charge brought against me I am perfectly innocent. O, this does support me. My Heavenly Father knows it, and however it may issue on earth, I hope to be acquitted when I, and those who are thirsting for my blood, stand at the tribunal of God. Commending you to God, and to the Word of his Grace, with earnest desires that His glory may be extended to earth's remotest bounds.

" I remain, my dear mother,

" Your affectionate son,

" WILLIAM KNIBB."

His mother never had this letter placed in her hands. She died before it arrived, but her last moments were brightened by the knowledge that her son was fighting the battle of freedom.

Meanwhile, Thomas Burchell was sailing from England on his return voyage in the *Garland Grove.* On his arrival in the harbour, he was peremptorily arrested, taken on board the *Blanche*, and conducted to the commodore's cabin. He was there informed that he would be allowed to walk as far as the mainmast, and that if he went beyond it he would be shot.

Yet Thomas Burchell was as innocent of any complicity with the insurrection as the waters beneath the ship which formed his prison.

The feeling against the Baptist Missionaries was most malignant. The *Jamaica Courant* said :—"Three Baptist preachers are now in custody. Shooting is too honourable a death for men whose conduct has occasioned so much bloodshed. There are fine hanging-woods in St. James' and Trelawney, and we do sincerely hope that the bodies of all the Methodist preachers who may be convicted of sedition may diversify the scene."

Shameful attempts were made to suborn witnesses against Mr. Burchell. Susan Mackenzie, a slave, but honourably known as "A great Baptist woman," was asked for evidence against him ; and because she would not, and could not give any, three men flogged her dreadfully, and she was then sent to the workhouse for medical treatment. She never walked upright again. A coloured man—George Spencer by name—refused to say a word against Mr. Burchell ; and he was taken into the open air, and shot dead !

But "the triumphing of the wicked" was short. The Battle for Freedom went on in England, and the day of Emancipation drew nigh. To promote its dawn, and the shedding forth of its blessed light, Thomas Burchell and William Knibb arrived in England, and the final struggle between Slavery and Freedom began.

Recently, on a calm Sunday afternoon, I walked down Kettering to Market Street, to look up at the window whence, early one morning, Knibb's mother, an invalid, having bade him farewell on his departure for the West Indies, called him back on his way to the coach, and said—" Remember, William, I would rather hear that you had perished in the sea, than that you had disgraced the cause you go to serve." Blessings on her memory— noble mother !   •

When the ship bearing William Knibb on board entered the Downs, in June, 1832, the pilot came on deck, and Knibb said, "Well, pilot, what news ?"   "The Reform Bill has passed." "Thank God," Knibb rejoined ; "now I'll have slavery down. I will never rest, day or night, till I see it destroyed root and branch."

On the 19th, William Knibb met the open meeting of the Committee of the Baptist Missionary Society, and had to endure a good many solemn counsels—and counsels not solemn—as to a temperate policy in reference to slavery ; and some present even ventured to advise silence !   The days of heroism are not past. William Knibb rose to his feet, and said :—" Myself, my wife, and my children are entirely dependent on the Baptist Missions ; we have landed without a shilling ; but if necessary I will walk barefoot through the kingdom, but what I will make known to the Christians in England what their brethren in Jamaica are suffering." The effect of these great words was manifest. Objectors sat dumb under their force.   Dr. Thomas Price, Charles Stovel, John Howard Hinton, and others, stood by William Knibb, and spoke words of cheer and love.

A grave crisis was at hand.   On Thursday, the 21st, the annual meeting of the Society was held in Spa Fields Chapel, (not Exeter Hall, as some have it) when Mr. Richard Foster, of Cambridge, presided.   Several speeches were made, but none touched the burning question of slavery.   Then came William Knibb, tall, ruddy, and fearless, and began his memorable speech.   " I appear," he said, in the course of his address, "as the advocate of 20,000 Baptists, who have no places of worship, no Sabbath, no houses of prayer, and I solemnly avow my belief that by far the greater part of those 20,000 will be flogged every time they are caught praying." As he went on speaking, his fervour and frankness increased, until at last the Rev. John Dyer pulled his coat tail. William Knibb wrenched himself away, and, in clarion tones, exclaimed, "I will speak. At the risk of my connection with the Society, and of all I hold dear, I will avow this. And if the friends of Missions will not hear me, I will turn and tell it to my God : nor will I desist till this greatest of curses is removed, and 'Glory to God in the highest' is inscribed on the British Flag."

From this sublime moment slavery was doomed. Thomas Burchell, William Knibb, Dr. Price, Dr. Hoby, Charles Stovel, William Brock, Frederick Trestrail, Dr. F. A. Cox, John Howard Hinton, and a host of other Baptist ministers, began a triumphant crusade against slavery, and other noble men, like Joseph Sturge, Joseph John Gurney, William Forster, Samuel Bowly, Robert Charlton, and George Thompson, "the eloquent orator," fought with them, and, at last, on the 1st of August, 1838, by the will of the English people,

The Slave was Free !

The previous day and night were most memorable in the history of Baptist Missions in Jamaica. A glorious page was then written in immortal lines. A transparency with the word Freedom shone in front of Knibb's chapel. Towards midnight the building was crowded with coloured people waiting for the moment of emancipation. Every heart palpitated with hope. Every eye blazed with expectancy. As midnight drew near, the clock began to strike twelve. Knibb, standing erect in his pulpit, pointed to the dial, and cried, "The hour is at hand ; the monster slavery is dying." When the last note of the clock sounded, he shouted, "The monster is dead ; the negro is free !" The excitement of the freed ones was

L

boundless.   They shouted aloud.   " Never," said Knibb, " did
I hear such a sound. The winds of freedom appeared to have been let
loose.   The very building shook at the strange, yet sacred joy."
The battle fought so nobly by Thomas Burchell and William
Knibb was won, and, from that day to this, England has owed
a debt to the Baptists for having purged the national flag from
the disgrace of protecting and perpetuating slavery.

What were the results of emancipation ? A competent writer
in the *The Year of Jubilee* says :—" The change that now took
place in the community was most remarkable. There was an
almost entire cessation of crime ; thousands of persons who had
been living in concubinage were married, vice was either abandoned or hidden, industry took the place of idleness, the schools
were filled, the places of worship could not contain the multitude
who crowded to hear the word of God, and large numbers gave
delightful evidence that they had not heard it in vain."

In August, 1839, in reply to an address from the Baptist
Missionaries, Sir Lionel Smith bore gratifying testimony to the
beneficial results of their labours, and to the conduct of the
people.   "On my assuming the government of this colony," he
said, " I strongly expressed my reliance on the whole body of
missionaries, in their high integrity of purpose, and in their loyal
principles. You more than realized all the benefits I expected
from your ministry, by raising the negroes from the mental
degradation of slavery to the cheering obligations of Christianity;
and they were thus taught that patient endurance of evil which
has so materially contributed to the general tranquillity. Even
with the aid of a vicious and well-paid press, both in England and
Jamaica—and, it may be presumed, some habitual confidence in
Jamaica juries—the enemies of your religion have never dared to
go to the proof of their audacious accusations against you.

" Gentlemen, the first year of freedom has passed away. What
were the forebodings of its enemies ?   Where are the vagrants ?
where the squatters ? where the injuries against proprietors or the

persons of white men? Out of the 800,000 oppressed slaves let loose in one day to equal rights and liberty, not a human being of that mass has committed himself in any of those dreaded offences.

"The admirable conduct of the peasantry in such a crisis has constituted a proud triumph to the cause of religion, and those who contributed to enlighten them in their moral duties, through persecutions, insults, and dangers, have deserved the regard and esteem of the good and just in all Christian countries."

Joseph John Gurney, the eminent Quaker, in his "Winter in the West Indies," wrote similar words in 1840. Thus he said :— "The Baptist missionaries in Jamaica, for many years past, have been the unflinching, untiring friends of the negro. No threats have daunted them, no insults or persecutions have driven them from the field. They are now reaping their reward in the devoted attachment of the people, and the increasingly prevalent acknowledgment of their integrity and usefulness." Speaking of the general improvement of the island, Mr. Gurney thus writes :— "But while these points are confessedly of high importance, there is a fourth, which at once embraces and outweighs them all,—I mean the diffusion of vital Christianity. I know that great apprehensions were entertained, especially in this country, on the cessation of slavery, that the negroes would break away at once from their masters and their ministers. But freedom has come, and while their masters have not been forsaken, their religious teachers have become dearer to them than ever. Under the banner of liberty the churches and meeting-houses have been enlarged and multiplied—the attendance has become regular and devout, the congregations have, in many cases, been more than doubled—above all, the *conversion of souls* (as we have reason to believe) has been going on to an extent never before known in these colonies. In a religious point of view, as I have before hinted, the wilderness in many places has begun to blossom as the rose ; ' instead of the thorn has come up the fir-tree, and instead of the briar has come up the myrtle-tree : and it shall be to the Lord for a name, for an everlasting sign that shall not be cut off.'"

William Knibb was a very affectionate man. The Rev. Phillip Saffery once told me a charming anecdote about him. Knibb went, accompanied by a friend, to have his portrait taken. As he sat in the chair waiting for the operation, his face became fixed and sombre. The artist said : " Think of something pleasant, Sir." A beautiful light beamed over Knibb's face, and the portrait was taken at once. His friend afterwards asked him what he thought about. " My wedding day," said Knibb.

The great eloquence of William Knibb at this period of his grand life is vividly described by the Rev. T. Pottinger. Speaking of a meeting held in Aberdeen, he says :—" The meeting was held in the place of worship at which the Rev. Mr. Simpson then preached, and which was capable of holding a large congregation. The platform was filled by magistrates, merchants, professors from both colleges, and ministers of all denominations in the city; while the building was crammed to excess by all ranks, eager to see and hear this champion of the negroes. Knibb felt that the occasion was a great one ; and his address that night surpassed all that his most devoted friends had anticipated. One tale of woe followed another in rapid succession, and either excited the feelings of the auditors to indignation or drew floods of tears from their eyes. The fire of eloquence which burst from the speaker may be said to have electrified the assembly. At one moment they were convulsed with laughter, and next they were sobbing aloud, or clenching their fists, ready to knock down the monster which the magician had conjured up in their midst; and, as when the great orator of Greece had delivered his orations, the Athenians were accustomed to say, 'Let us march against Philip !' so, when the man of God had finished his noble speech on that memorable occasion, the multitude seemed to say, ' Let us march against slavery !' On the platform near me sat a gentleman, I believe either a professor in one of the colleges or a minister in one of the parish churches, whose spirit was deeply stirred within him. As the speaker continued to expose and denounce the abominations of colonial slavery, he made free use of a large stick which he held in his hand ; but at length, after one of the finest bursts of eloquence to which I ever listened, he suddenly jumped on his feet, exclaiming, ' This is Demosthenes !'

" Thirteen years at least have passed away since that meeting rang the knell of slavery ; but even now the speaker, the excited multitude, the shouts of applause, the tears of grief, and the whole scene, are as fresh in my recollection as they were that night, when I went home wondering at what I had heard."

It may be asked—whether the Baptist missionaries deserve all the praise we have accorded to them ? I reply : 1. The clergy of the Church of England in Jamaica, with one exception, took no part in the battle for freedom ; and, 2. The want of sympathy felt by the missionaries of other denominations was universally manifested.*

Let not the Baptist denomination regard its work in relation to slavery as completely accomplished. Slavery still exists in the world. In Morocco there are 137,000 slaves. Persia holds 200,000 in bondage. In Egypt, 850,000 human beings groan in their chains. And in Turkey, 1,500,000 souls endure the misery of being bought and sold, outraged and worked to death.

There is therefore a loud cry sounding through the heavens, calling upon us to " remember them that are in bonds." Let us give most earnest heed to that pathetic and solemn summons, and seek in every way we can to give liberty to the captive, for

'Tis liberty alone that gives the flower
Of life its lustre and perfume,
And we are weeds without it."

We do therefore implore the young men of our Churches espe-

---

* See Knibb's Life, page 551.

cially to study this great question of slavery, become the worthy
followers of Burchell and Knibb, Sturge and Gurney, and, avoiding
trivial pursuits, keep in mind that—

" 'Tis not for man to trifle; life is brief
    And sin is here ;
Our age is but the falling of a leaf,
    A dropping tear.
We have not time to sport away the hours:
All must be earnest in a world like ours.
Not many lives, but only one have we,
    One, only one.
How sacred should that one life ever be,
    That narrow span !
Day after day filled up with blessed toil,
Hour after hour still bringing in new spoil."

BAPTISTS AND THE TEMPERANCE REFORM;

BY

REV. DAWSON BURNS, M.A.

———◆———

PRECEDING lectures have exhibited the relation which, as Baptists, we consider ourselves to hold to the Primitive Church ; to a scriptural polity and creed ; and to the shining ranks of martyrs, confessors, teachers, missionaries, and philanthropists, who "have kept the faith" and entered on the great reward. It is left for me to show the relation sustained by Baptists to the Temperance Reform in the past ; their connection with it at the present time ; and the place they ought to take in its future prosecution and successes.

I.—THE PAST.

As there were Religious Reformers before the Reformation of the sixteenth century, so there were Baptists who, prior to the Temperance movement, were in sympathy with its principles and aims. The greatest epic poet of England, and the greatest poet the world has seen for 600 years—John Milton—was a Baptist in conviction, as is clear from both his prose and poetic works. He was also most abstemious in his habits ; and in two of his lesser poems, "Comus" and "Samson Agonistes," he has depicted the degradation arising from sensual indulgence, and the virtue and beauty

of a temperance finding its fitting and fullest expression in abstinence from all intoxicants.

During the eighteenth century, a protest was made by some of
the wisest and best of men against the use of intoxicating liquors.
Among these were John Wesley, Dr. Johnson, John Howard,* and
several medical men of distinction. Of the latter, in America, was
Dr. Benjamin Rush, whose attacks on the use of ardent spirits
attracted considerable attention. Whether connected or not with
this crusade I cannot say, but at that time there was living in
Newport, Rhode Island, a Baptist minister, familiarly known as
"Father Thurston," whose small stipend compelled him to work
with his hands, as did the Apostle Paul. Father Thurston, however, was not a tentmaker, but a cooper, a trade somewhat flourishing at Newport, as it was then engaged in the West Indian trade and
furnished many casks for the transit of rum. But Father Thurston
having a dislike to this abuse of industry, would not make casks,
and limited his labour to the production of vessels that were
otherwise applied. It is believed, says the biographer of Dr.
Channing, that this example of adhesion to temperance principle,
made an impression on the mind of the young student residing in
Newport, and prepared his way for a subsequent union with the
Temperance Reform, and advocacy of its claims.† Honour to
Father Thurston ! We may be sure that if he would not use his
hands to fabricate casks for holding rum, he did not turn his own
body into a vessel for its reception.

About the same time, a young Baptist minister at Cambridge,
in England, was becoming known as one of the most eloquent
preachers of the day ; and according to Dr. Stanley, the Dean of

---

* John Howard, though not a Baptist, was for some time a trustee and
member of the "Old Meeting" at Bedford, whose line of ministers comprised
the "glorious dreamer," John Bunyan.

† See life of Dr. Channing, by his nephew, W. H. Channing, Vol. I.
p. 32. This incident was referred to in felicitous terms, by Dr. James
Martineau, in his address at the Channing Celebration in St. James's Hall,
April 9th, 1880.

Westminster, the greatest preacher England has ever had was this same Baptist minister, Robert Hall. In the early period of his ministry at Cambridge, Mr. Hall was acquainted with a gentleman who, when calling upon him, was accustomed to ask for "a little brandy and water." Mr. Hall knew that this habit was his bane, and resolved upon "a strong effort for his rescue." Accordingly, when the gentleman called one day and asked for a glass of brandy and water, Mr. Hall said, "Call things by their right names, and you shall have as much as you please." He answered, "Why, don't I employ the right name? I ask for a glass of brandy and water." Mr. Hall replied, "This is the current, but not the appropriate name; ask for a glass of liquid fire and distilled damnation, and you shall have a gallon!" Did ever Temperance "fanatic" utter a more fiery and scathing denunciation of alcoholic liquor? By the side of it, how pale is even the definition of alcohol as the "Devil in solution!" a definition credited to Dr. Richardson, and adopted by Mr. Walter, M.P. It is pleasing to know that though the gentleman was at first disposed to be angry, he received the rebuke in good part, and, said Mr. Hall, "from that time ceased to take brandy and water."*

Early in 1826 the Temperance Reform began in earnest by the formation of the American Temperance Society, in Park Street Church, Boston, United States. This church (Congregational) I have visited as a pilgrim, and have stood with deep emotion within the building where, fifty-five years ago, this mighty Reform was born and cradled. The Christian churches of America were generally quick in their replies to the call for help and service, and the Baptists were not last, or least active in their allegiance to this cause of patriotism and humanity. The Temperance movement crossed the Atlantic in 1829, and for several years was advocated on the basis of abstinence from distilled

---

* Works of Robert Hall, edited by Dr. Gregory, vol. vi. pp. 23-4.

spirits, the use of fermented liquors being optional.   Rev. Dr. F. A. Cox, of Hackney, was on the Committee of the British and Foreign Temperance Society, and one of its early agents, and for a long time its Secretary was Rev. Owen Clarke, of Vernon Chapel, Pentonville.   But in 1832 the principle of Total Abstinence from all intoxicating liquors was vigorously advocated, and in a few years the old societies were mostly reconstituted on this basis, and many others were established.

In this work, English Baptists were conspicuous by their presence and energy.   In the North of England, where this reformed Reformation originated, it found two able and zealous allies in John and Joseph Andrew, of Leeds.   Mr. John Andrew, who became a Baptist, was Secretary of the British Temperance Association, and both in Leeds, where he resided, and throughout that whole region, was recognized as one of the leaders of the cause, and he still lives to rejoice in its larger triumphs.   In Manchester laboured the Rev. Francis Beardsall, minister of Oak Street General Baptist Chapel, one of the first used for the promotion of total abstinence.   Mr. Beardsall, besides preaching and lecturing, edited the *Temperance Star*, and gave expression to views on the Bible Wine question which brought ridicule upon him, but which have since found favour with the most distinguished scholars. Wishing to reside in America, he took passage in a sailing-ship, but he died on the voyage, and his body was committed to the Atlantic depths, but his courageous devotion to the Temperance movement, in its struggling days, deserves to be had in undying remembrance.   From 1836 to 1840, the Temperance Reform had few devoted supporters among the Christian ministers of London, but some of that few were Baptists, including the Rev. J. Woodard, of Ilford, deceased; Rev. J. Sears, of Camberwell, still living; and the Rev. J. Stevenson, M.A., of Borough Road Chapel, deceased. More prominent in Baptist circles, and both men of remarkable ability, were Rev. Charles Stovel and Rev. J. Howard Hinton, M.A.   The former survives, and retains for the good cause an affection which he displayed forty years ago by speeches that delighted and convinced. Mr. Hinton was less decided and steadfast; but as one of the adjudicators of the prize of £100 for the best essay on the Temperance subject, in 1839, he gave his vote in favour of "Anti-Bacchus," and thus probably encouraged the author (Rev. B. Parsons) to print his essay—one of the most useful and valuable contributions to Temperance literature ever published, though less elaborate and lore-laden than its successful rival, "Bacchus," by Dr. Grindrod. Within this period, however (1836-40), another Baptist minister was labouring in a Western London parish; and having been associated while in Scotland with the old Temperance Society, he entered into the Total Abstinence movement with the full ardour of an enthusiastic nature, and until the day of his death he was constant in his devotion to its interests. He edited for years Temperance periodicals; lectured and preached to numerous audiences in every part of the kingdom; entered heartily into every department of Temperance effort; delivered one of the inaugural discourses of the United Kingdom Alliance in 1853, and travelled far and wide to introduce its principles to public notice. In his own chapel he commenced the series of annual Temperance sermons, thirty-five of which he was privileged to deliver; and in 1841 began to celebrate the Lord's Supper in unfermented wine. No other Christian minister of any denomination ever did more to advance the Temperance cause than did he; and I have no hesitation, in the exercise of an unbiassed judgment, in declaring, that among the highest and brightest names on the roll of Temperance pioneers and champions, stands, and ever will stand, the name of Dr. Jabez Burns. It is no flattery to say this. He has gone where the voice of the flatterer is never heard, and where the works of the just appear before the Judge of All, to testify that they were done for His glory and according to His holy will.

In Wales, the Temperance Reform found many friends among the Christian ministry—Baptists not excepted, who imitated in this respect the example of men like Christmas Evans, one of the greatest preachers Wales has known. That "Son of Thunder" was a strong advocate of Temperance, and once remarked that when he gave up his occasional glass he thought he was offering up a fat ox from the stall, but afterwards discovered that it was only a rat ! This comparison rightly illustrates the imaginary nature of the sacrifice which persons make by the surrender of strong drink. To get rid of the "rats" can scarcely be classed among the acts for which the title of heroic benevolence may be claimed !

In Scotland, the Temperance movement of 1829-35 met with the active and able co-operation of Mr. Robert Kettle, a Baptist merchant of Glasgow, who entered with the same zeal into the Total Abstinence enterprise. He was the first editor of the *Scottish Temperance Journal*, and was appointed President of the Scottish Temperance League in 1848. A worthy fellow-labourer, who has recently joined him in the heavenly home, was the Rev. Dr. Paterson, of Glasgow, President of the Baptist Theological Institution of Scotland, and editor of some of the principal periodicals of the Scottish Temperance League.

It is only possible to name some out of many others who rendered cordial help to the Temperance cause in different parts of the kingdom at this period :—Rev. C. H. Rae, of Birmingham ; Rev. C. M. Birrell, of Liverpool ; Rev. T. W. Matthews, of Boston ; Rev. Dr. Evans, of Scarborough ; Hon. and Rev. Baptist Noel, of London ; Rev. Francis Johnstone, of Edinburgh ; and the Rev. James Wells, of London.

Besides the work done by the fore-named, a glance at the early records of the Temperance Reform gives evidence of the eminent service rendered to it by Baptists, most of whom have passed away, but some of whom continue "unto this present." Mr. John Meredith, who had retired from business in the country, and removed to London, was one of the Secretaries of the New British and Foreign Temperance Society ; a most diligent and laborious

Temperance organizer in the South of London, and Superintendent of the Metropolitan Temperance Mission, which for a time employed a staff of agents. Mr. Meredith was very successful in his private persuasions to the adoption of total abstinence, and being aided by an excellent wife, he had the joy of seeing his whole family attached to the cause he long and lovingly promoted. Mr. James Balfour was very assiduous and popular for a series of years as a Temperance Agent and Missionary (doing an excellent work in France in 1845, among the English workmen employed on the Havre and Rouen Railway), and in his 85th year retains a lively interest in all that concerns the Temperance Reform. The late Rev. T. J. Messer for more than a generation and a quarter consistently, and persistently, advocated the Temperance principle from the pulpit and the platform. Mr. Thomas Smeeton was for years an energetic and able lecturing agent ; and afterwards when settled in Ipswich, edited the *Temperance Recorder,* and wrote a prize essay for young men. Sixteen years have passed since the death of the Rev. Jabez Tunnicliff, of Leeds, General Baptist Minister; by whom the first Band of Hope was formed in this country, in the August of 1847. Mr. Tunnicliff continued through his life to be actively concerned in the Temperance training of the young.

It is but recently that the movement has lost in Mr. Jabez Inwards an advocate of portly presence, and very popular address, whose voice constantly, and pen occasionally, were plied for forty years on behalf of the Teetotalism in which he believed with all his heart.

Having as a youth embraced Temperance principles in Newcastle-on-Tyne, and having proved their worth in Home Missionary work in Norwich, and St. Giles', London, the Rev. G. W. M'Cree, now the pastor of the Borough-road General Baptist Church, is ever at home, in any place, in commending the Temperance Reform, to which by his lectures, speeches, and writings, he has rendered signal service.* For thirteen years Mr. M'Cree was widely known and appreciated as the Secretary of the United Kingdom Band of Hope Union. An early Temperance Worker in London, and author of a useful Catechism, Mr. J. P. Parker, may claim a place in this list of Baptist Temperance Worthies. The late Mr. Simeon Smithard employed with success the charms of music, both to attract assemblies and to win them to the cause he loved. In the Rev. Samuel Couling the Temperance Movement acknowledges a recorder of its progress and an acceptable contributor to its periodical literature ; and as the author of an illustrated work, " The Worship of Bacchus," and an earnest Band of Hope worker, Mr. Ebenezer Clarke, a Baptist deacon, ought not to pass unnamed. Honourable mention must also be made of the late Mr. Walter Ludbrook as the publisher of a series of " London Temperance Tracts," and an energetic friend of all Temperance measures. Popular as a lecturer, and still more popular as a writer, is Mr. J. W. Kirton, author of " Buy your own Cherries," the " Four Pillars of Temperance," &c.; and he is still adding to the stores of knowledge by which converts are to be won, and abstainers edified and confirmed. Who has not heard of the cosmopolitan Excursionist, Thomas Cook ? But all the world does not know that he is a General Baptist, and one of the principal supporters of the Baptist mission in Rome ; and that for forty-four years he has been a zealous advocate of Temperance by the use of the pen and press. From him proceeded the scheme by which a cluster of mean houses, including a public-house, was swept away and replaced by a block of handsome buildings comprising the Temperance Hall and Hotel in Leicester. It is also an interesting fact, that his Excursionist system had its germ in

---

* The Conference of Temperance Workers held Feb. 17, 1871, from which has sprung the London Temperance Hospital, was convened by two Baptists, one of whom was Mr. M'Cree, and the other the writer of this. Name known far and near as the Metropolitan Superintendent of the United Kingdom Alliance, and author of some most valuable works on Temperance.
[*Ed.*

the arrangements he made during successive years for a temperance excursion from Leicester to adjacent places of rural or historic fame.

About the year 1836, an officer in the 13th Light (Native) Infantry Regiment in India was noted for his Christian character and Temperance principles. He sought, and not in vain, to show that piety and abstinence are contributive to the best qualities of a British officer. He took part in the invasion of Afghanistan in 1842, and was besieged with Sir Robert Sale in Jellalabad, where the health and general conduct of the troops were remarkable, and were attributed by Sir Robert Sale to the absence of strong drink. From grade to grade he rose as years went by, and the time arrived when his matured abilities found a theatre worthy of them all. The Indian Sepoy Mutiny began in the June of 1857, and it seemed for a while as if our Indian Empire was about to become "the baseless fabric of a vision, leaving not a wrack behind." Hope revived when it became known that a body of troops was put under the command of this able General. His march from Allahabad to Cawnpore was a march of battles and of victories. But his destination was Lucknow, where a British garrison, with women and children, had been besieged in the Residency for many weeks. At length came the glad news that the relieving force, small as it was, had thrown itself into Lucknow's narrow streets crowded with foes, and had entered the Residency, where it was itself beleagured, but ensuring the safety of the half-despairing defenders, till an army under Sir Colin Campbell advanced and opened up a way to the Residency amidst the ruins of the city. The meeting of the Generals has become historical. One name, however, was more in men's minds and hearts than any other. It wanted not the distinction of a baronetcy conferred on the dying soldier to mark the national sense of the high position he had gained ; and when the news of his decease arrived, I well remember how the tribute of a nation's grief was paid to the unblemished Christian hero—Baptist and abstainer—Sir Henry Havelock !

It has ever been admitted that woman's influence in the Temperance Reform is of vast importance, and would be decisive, were it cast at once and wholly in its favour. Many Christian women have done excellent work for this great cause ; but if there were one palm alone to be assigned, little doubt would exist but that it ought to be awarded to a Baptist. She had lived for years in obscurity, but having embraced the principle of Abstinence, her talents were quickly recognised and called into exercise both as a writer and a speaker. In a short time she had edited two Temperance publications, refuted a medical opponent, and published a "Garland of Water Flowers." As co-editor of the *Temperance Journal* she wrote a series of Temperance Tales, and issued the " Juvenile Abstainer," which, under the later name of " Morning Dew Drops," is a standard book for young Abstainers. In subsequent years, her remarkable abilities as a lecturer on literary and other topics were called into constant request, and her pen threw off, loom-like, products, rich in colour, and beautiful in design ; but her heart and life remained consecrated to Temperance work ; and when, in the July of 1878, she passed away, it was unanimously confessed that of all the women who had nobly directed noble gifts to the service of this Reform, none could compare with Mrs. Clara Lucas Balfour. Her Temperance Addresses had a pathos all their own, and her Temperance Works constitute a library abounding in whatever can gratify the taste, and elevate the mind.

II.—THE PRESENT.

Towards the latter end of 1859, I drew up, at the instance of the National Temperance League Committee, an address to Baptist ministers on the Temperance Question. This received the signature of 224 ministers and thirty-six students. Some years later, a second address of a similar kind received the names of about 260 ministers. But in 1881, the names of 537 ministers, and of 228 students (out of 287—four-fifths of the whole number) are recorded as Total Abstainers. This is gratifying numerical progress, and it proves that, as a denomination, we have been changing for the better our attitude to the Temperance Reform. Nor is this all. Omitting those living Baptists who have been previously referred to as Temperance workers, there is encouragement to be drawn from the position and influence of many of the men among us who have taken their place on the side of Total Abstinence. Who preaches by voice and print to so large a congregation as the Rev. C. H. Spurgeon, or has done a greater work for the training of a ministry fervent in spirit and serving the Lord ? And whether speaking in his own name, or under that of John Ploughman, Mr. Spurgeon's words for Temperance are ever welcome, and ever weighty. Among the heads of Collegiate Institutions may be named, Rev. Dr. Thomas, Ex-President of Pontypool College; Rev. G. T. Rooke, LL.B., of Rawdon College, Bradford ; and Dr. Culross, of the Theological Institution, Glasgow. Among ministers and pastors of acknowledged eminence, and who have been called to offices of trust and consequence in connection with our body, may be named, Rev. S. H. Booth, Rev. W. Brock, Rev. J. P. Chown, Rev. John Clifford, M.A., LL.B. (Editor of the *General Baptist Magazine*), Rev. J. H. Cooke (editor of the *Freeman*), Rev. Dr. Stanford, Rev. Dr. Stock, and Rev. C. Williams; while of others, including younger brethren of power and promise, there is a goodly and interesting company in sympathy with the Temperance Cause. Of these, Rev. J. Fletcher is an example. Justly esteemed as a successful evangelist and pastor, while pursuing his business as a merchant, is Mr. W. P. Lockhart, of Liverpool. Consistent, too, in utterance and example, has been Mr. Henry Varley, so widely-known for his evangelistic labours. The officers of our churches are still furnishing, as they have done, valuable assistance in the diffusion of Temperance principles. The late Mr. J. S. Wright, M.P., was one of these, and has left a filial successor in the same good work. Other examples are supplied by Mr. W. S. Caine, M.P. (President of the Baptist Total

Abstinence Association) ; Mr. G. W. Anstie, of Devizes ; Mr. Peter Spence, J.P., senior deacon of Dr. MacLaren's Church, Manchester ; Mr. Alderman Strachan, of South Shields ; Mr. Cory, of Cardiff ; Messrs. Bacon and Waland, of London ; with a long list of others who have "earned to themselves a good degree" in this particular labour of love. The medical profession is now, by means of some of its members, nobly assisting the Temperance Reform, and Dr. Pearce, of Plymouth, is a Baptist representative of enlightened medical sentiment and practice on this subject.

The United Kingdom Band of Hope Union, one of our largest Temperance Institutions, had a Baptist, Mr. Stephen Shirley, for its principal founder, who is also its present chairman ; and at a still earlier date, the Band of Hope movement in London owed very much to the zeal and toil of Mr. J. H. Esterbrooke, who is a Baptist. The National Temperance League has pursued, and is still pursuing, a career of distinguished Temperance activity and usefulness ; and none can doubt that it owes much of both to the tact and ability of its indefatigable secretary, Mr. Robert Rae, who is a Baptist. Foreign Missions move the hearts and stimulate the hopes of the Christian world. Every missionary should be a Total Abstainer, both for his own sake, and for the sake of the people among whom he lives and labours. Not a few Baptist missionaries are so, but to no other missionary, of any denomination, has it yet fallen to effect so much good for the British Army as the Rev. J. Gelson Gregson, has been privileged to bring about by means of the Soldiers' Total Abstinence Society of India. About 9,000 English soldiers there are members of Regimental Temperance Societies, and the benefits resulting from this Temperance propaganda in the army, called forth, some time ago, emphatic commendation from Lord Napier of Magdala, when Commander-in-Chief, and from the Earl of Northbrook, when Governor-General of India.

III.—THE FUTURE.

In regard to the Temperance Reform, "can" and "should" are terms of co-ordinate meaning, and as it cannot be pretended that Baptists have done all they can in behalf of the Total Abstinence cause, it is proper to enquire, What can, and, therefore, ought they to do for its promotion? Speaking generally, it may be replied that they can do at least what is done by the Baptists of America, both in the United States and in Canada, viz., practise Abstinence from intoxicating drinks. As early as 1830, the annual Conference of Baptists of Nova Scotia passed a resolution strongly recommending the Temperance cause to the united and vigorous support of the Baptists of that province.

At the present time, personal Abstinence is understood to be the rule among Baptists of all sections across the Atlantic, whether ministers, officers, or private members. Men and women professing godliness, profess to abstain from all intoxicating liquors, and that the overwhelming majority are true to their profession, I do not doubt. At the Free-Will Baptist Triennial and Centennial Conference, which I attended in the July of 1880, the strongest resolutions were passed on this question, and it was clear that the practice and promotion of Abstinence were regarded as a Christian duty not to be violated with a conscience void of offence to God or man. So it has been for many years; and I may here diverge for a moment to observe, that both the physical and spiritual results have been found of a self-rewarding character. As to the former, it may suffice to state that of seventy-five ministers who had died since the last Triennial Conference, the average age at death was 69½; and, but for the decease of a few younger men, the average would have been nearer 80 than 70. Now I do not see why American Baptists should be in advance of British Baptists in this, or any other, track of Christian philanthropy, and I am sure than if even every Baptist were a Total Abstainer, not one would have done more than adopt a course at once beneficial to himself, and contributive to his greater usefulness in the family, society, and the Church. But again—as it seems to me—we may, and ought, as Baptists to take action on this great question in three ways : 1st, Denominationally ; 2ndly, Congregationally ; 3rdly, Educationally. Let me venture a few words on each.

1st. *Denominational Action.*—Resolutions, more or less, of a Temperance character have been passed by the General Baptist Association, and several County Associations ; but owing to our form of union being different to that of Methodists and Presbyterians, there would be difficulties in the way of direct denominational action on behalf of the Temperance Reform. Yet, as the Baptists do unite voluntarily for various objects, there is no reason why they should not add the Temperance question to the others. This conjoint action has been rendered easy by the formation of the Baptist Total Abstinence Association in May, 1874. Membership in it is provided for in the case of ministers, students, and officers of churches, by forwarding the name and address of any such person being an Abstainer ; and in the case of other abstaining Baptists, by a subscription of 2s. 6d. a year. I have before referred to the number of ministers and students whose names have been so transmitted, but it is curious to find that the officers and others who are entered as members do not exceed (by the last report) 325 in number. It is probable that the Abstaining officers of Baptist churches are three or four-fold greater than the ministers, so that the figures in the report witness to a lamentable remissness in forwarding the names of abstaining officers. Cannot this be corrected ? Each Abstaining minister might assist to supply the deficiency. And as to the small subscription which others have to pay to be enrolled as members, it can offer no hindrance where the heart is interested in the work.* In one particular this denominational Society has set others an

---

* Mr. J. T. Sears, the Secretary of the Baptist Total Abstinence Association, will be glad to receive the names of Baptist Abstainers addressed to him at 232, Southampton Street, Camberwell Road, London, S.E.

example by the appointment of a travelling and organizing agent, Rev. W. L. Lang.

2ndly. *Congregational Action.*—A Temperance organisation should exist in each Congregation, holding its meetings from time to time, and existing for the good of the neighbourhood in which the Church is situated. The minister, if a Total Abstainer, would be the appropriate president ; and, in any case, there would be a natural identification of the Temperance Movement with the work of the Congregation. To sustain this action, official encouragement will be valuable, but not indispensable. An active Committee would keep the fire burning and make it spread.

3rdly. *Educational Action.*—At proper seasons, the value of Total Abstinence should be impressed on Sunday School children, and a vigilant teacher would find many opportunities of doing this without diverging from the lessons of the day. Then a Band of Hope, either distinct from the Sunday School or in connection with it, should be formed, and suitable exercises provided. The Wesleyan Conference passed, some years ago, a resolution, that a Band of Hope should be attached to every chapel in the Connexion, and though this rule has not been absolutely carried out, the Bands of Hope reported in August, 1880, numbered 1,831, with a membership of 178,207. There are few who object to the training of the young in Temperance principles and practice, and it is by the gathering in of the young, and their preservation, that very much of the future progress of the cause is to be secured. As Baptists we ought to take a part, and a leading one, in such means for saving the rising race from the paths of the destroyer. On one point I would be explicit. The Temperance Reform is not to be forwarded, much less accomplished, by one method of operation. All the causes of drinking and drunkenness must be attacked, if the conquest is to be gained; and, therefore, in the field of legislation, Baptists should be conspicuous for their energy and ardour. Sunday Closing Bills, restrictive proposals, and, above all, Local Option ought to be demanded by Baptists with one mind and voice. We have often witnessed against tyranny and oppression, but the archives of history may be ransacked in vain for an example of greater oppression than that which is presented under our licensing system. A small body of magistrates license, from year to year, a traffic which is the nation's plague, and no legal power of prevention is yet afforded. By a law of Local Option this would be remedied, and the inhabitants of districts would enjoy the blessed liberty of shaking themselves free from a weight which neither they nor their fathers have been able to bear. A prelate of the Church of England once ventured to say he would rather see England free than sober. I have replied to him by saying, what I now repeat, that England cannot be free without being sober ; that she is not now free, because under the power of brewers, distillers, and liquor sellers ; and that Local Option, by making it possible for her to be sober, would inaugurate an era of freedom from social suffering and demoralization, which would place her civil and political liberties on a firmer basis, and make her great and prosperous beyond all present possibility.

If I am asked to define the Temperance position of Baptists as compared with other prominent denominations, I do not pretend to exquisite precision, but negatively I may say—we are not first, and, more encouragingly, that we are not last. Perhaps, as to relative numbers and influence, the Society of Friends (usually called Quakers) takes the lead in England. The Methodist bodies come next; one of the lesser—the Bible Christians—deserving to be placed beside the Friends. The English Presbyterians follow ; then the Congregationalists; then "we Baptists"; next, the New Church and Unitarians may be linked for this purpose, if for no other ; and the rear is brought up by the Established Church. Looking, however, at the matter not numerically, but organisationally, I am not sure whether the Church of England may not claim to be foremost in the work, for though its dual basis admits large numbers into the Church of England Temperance Society who are not abstainers, it is to be remembered that every local

society has a total abstinence section, which is generally the most
active and numerous; and that the number of abstainers both
among clergy and laity is rapidly increasing. Late in moving,
the Church of England has made steady progress in the last few
years, and Nonconformist bodies must look to their laurels if they
desire them to be retained. For myself, I wish the utmost success
to all Christian Churches in this Christian work, though I should
like our own denomination to be just a little ahead of every other!
The others, I am sure, will pardon this touch of special affection.
Sure I am that the whole Church would find enough to do in
breaking down the power of the drinking system. And what a
heart-rejoicing spectacle will it be when Christ's Church is
combined against the antichrist of Alcohol! Oh, to see the
armies of the faithful casting themselves with one accord upon the
sources and defences of intemperance, and by their irresistible
onset sweeping them away! It is perfectly certain that the forces
by which the present system is kept in operation are so potent
that the need for action to counterweight and remove them is
absolutely imperative. Ignorance, Apathy, Appetite, Greed,
Custom, are not opponents to be despised, and they are all in
league to sustain and extend the manufacture, sale, and use of
intoxicating liquors, and to thwart efforts for the abolition of the
drinking system. Who shall enlighten the ignorant, stir the
apathetic, persuade the victims of appetite to deny themselves,
and put away evil customs, and defy the "vested interests" of
the traffickers in strong drink? Christians must be looked for,
and relied upon, to do this, if it is to be done at all; and that it
ought to be done, and must be done, if the country is to be saved,
who that has studied this social problem can doubt for a moment?
If it is arduous, are not Christians to be expected to show hardness
as good soldiers of Jesus Christ? If it is heroic, who should be
heroes but those who say, "We can do all things through
Christ who strengtheneth us"? And, brethren, if we are Baptists,
we are Christians—Christians first—and ought to be eager to

make our Christian calling and election sure. If we claim, as Baptists, to trace our origin to the primitive Church, let us prove our relationship by primitive good works.   If we claim a Scriptural polity and creed, let us remember that these need vitalizing by the spirit of love and zeal, without which ecclesiastical organisations are but painted pageants, and dogmatic standards, tinkling cymbals.   If we claim, as we justly may, that Baptists are in no small numbers to be found in the shining ranks of martyrs, confessors, teachers, missionaries, and philanthropists, let us be emulous of a place in the ranks of Temperance reformers, who have set their hands to a work of unparalleled social importance, and one profoundly connected with the prosperity of the Church and the salvation of men.

Doing what we might, and with all our might, who can predict the consequences, both immediate and ultimate? This we know, that they will be gladdening and glorious ; and that we may then consistently, and believingly, pray " Thy Kingdom come !" And then the Kingdom of God will come with a power and a brightness for which the world has long been waiting !

NOTES.

NOTES.

Note A.—The Origin of Infant Baptism

Is involved in some obscurity. Pressensé, a recent Pædobaptist witness, says, in his *Apostolic Age*, pp. 374-376, " Faith was required from every candidate for baptism. The idea never occurred to Paul that baptism might be divorced from faith—the sign from the thing signified." " Christian baptism is not to be received any more than faith, by right of inheritance. This is the great reason why we cannot believe that it was administered in the Apostolic age to little children. No positive fact sanctioning the practice can be adduced from the New Testament : the historical proofs alleged are in no way conclusive." The first century is without a solitary note in favour of infant baptism, and the whole genius of the practical and personal Christianity of that age forcibly precludes the idea of its appearance.

What is the witness of the *second* century to infant baptism ? The passage in Irenæus (Heresies, Book II. cxxii. §4) is thus given by Neander (Church History, Bohn's edition, vol. I. 431) " He (Christ) came to redeem all by Himself, all who through Him are born again unto God—infants, little children, boys, young men and old. Therefore He passed through every age ; for the infants He became an infant, sanctifying the infants ; among the little children He became a little child, to sanctify those who are of this age, and at the same time to present to them an example of piety, uprightness, and obedience ; among the young men, He became a young man, that He might set them an example, and sanctify them to the Lord."

Now the accomplished Neander, though saying, " There does not appear to be any reason for deriving infant baptism from an apostolical institution," yet claims the above passage as a witness in favour of infant baptism, and thus cites the authority of the greatest bishop of the second century for the existence of that rite at so early a date. Is this interpretation right ?

Pressensé (Heresy and Christian Doctrine, 399), like Hagenbach, asserts that it is "a purely gratuitous supposition." Let us look for ourselves. (1.) Clearly Irenæus is *not* directly or even indirectly discoursing of baptism. It is not in the text or context. It does not lie in the course of the drift of his teaching.

(2.) It is obvious that he is expounding that grand Johannine conception of "the Word made flesh," that the Incarnation is the sanctification of universal human life, omitting no individual of the race, and no stage in the life of any individual. Christ was the "perfect man, that is to say, man perfectly united to God."* "He recapitulates, as it were, in Himself the whole human race. He is the head of mankind; representing not only all generations, but all ages; for He redeemed childhood, youth, and mature age, by being Himself successively child, youth, and full-grown man."† It is of the effect of the *Incarnation* and not of baptism that he is speaking.

(3.) It ought to go for something that the idea of the intrinsic virtue of a *sacrament* had not yet gained a secure footing. Pressensé says, that in speaking of the primitive Church, we must set aside all notions of sacramental grace by which the operation of God is assimilated to the arts of magic,‡ and Bunsen affirms that such conceptions of Divine grace were borrowed from the lustrations of decaying paganism;§ and the former goes so far as to affirm, that "the essential feature of the institutions of the second and *third* centuries is this very predominance of the baptism of adult catechumens with their foregoing training." Of Justin Martyr, the Greek philosopher of Samaria, who from a decided Platonist became a Christian about the year 132, and was martyred in Rome for refusing to sacrifice to the gods about the year 168, he says :—"The notion of sacrament is scarcely at all developed in his writings. He attaches much importance to baptism; he opposes it to natural birth, which is a necessity, and brings us into a state of ignorance, whilst baptism renders us children of God by the forgiveness of our sins. But it produces these results only by means of a living faith; it is not similar to the washings of the Jews, for all the waves of the sea could not wash away sin. It purifies only by faith in Christ crucified. Baptism is salutary only to the repentant sinner; then it becomes a spring of life, and deserves to be called a source of light: but this is entirely due to the truth which it calls to mind. Justin does not mention

---

* "Hœres" III. 33, V. 1.   † Ibid III. 20, II. 39.
‡ Apostolic Age, 373.   § Hippolytus II. 127.

the baptism of infants, but speaks only of their being instructed."[*] We may therefore warrantably affirm, that it was highly improbable Irenæus had infant baptism in his mind when he wrote of the wide and glorious effects of the Incarnation. The conclusion, long-established, and recognised; that infant baptism did not originate in the *second* century will require other evidence than this before it is disturbed.

But that it had arisen in the *third* century is evident (*a*) from "The Constitutions of the Egyptian Church" (II. 46), which direct thus, "Let any one of them who can speak, speak when required in the service. If he cannot speak, let the parents answer for him;" (*b*) from Origen (born, 184 A.D.; died, 253) who "connected the baptism of infants with his favourite theory of a full antecedent to an earthly existence;" (*c*) and Tertullian, who "complained bitterly of the abuse which had so soon followed on this practice."

To sum-up, there is not a jot of evidence in favour of the existence of infant baptism in the *first* century; the witness is exceedingly dubious as to its origin in the second; but that it was recognised by some, and opposed by others, in the third, there is no doubt.

Note B.—The Primitive Mode of Baptism.

Is Sprinkling New Testament baptism? Let Dean Stanley answer—"There can be no question that the original form of baptism—the very meaning of the word—was complete immersion in the deep baptismal waters; and that for at least four centuries any other form was either unknown, or regarded, unless in the case of danger or illness, as an exceptional, almost a monstrous case. To this form the Eastern church still rigidly adheres; and the most illustrious and venerable portion of it, that of the Byzantine Empire, absolutely repudiates and ignores any other mode of administration as essentially invalid. The Latin church has wholly altered the mode, and with the two exceptions of the cathedral of Milan and the sect of the Baptists, a few drops of water are now the Western substitute for the three-fold plunge into the rushing rivers or the wide baptisteries of the East."—*Hist. East. Ch.* Lec. I.

Add to this Professor Maine's testimony, also a learned Pædobaptist,— " It may be honestly asked by some, Was immersion the primitive form of baptism; and if so, what then? As to the question of fact, the testimony

---

[*] Life and Practice of the Early Church, 21.

is ample and decisive. No matter of church history is clearer. The
evidence is all one way, and all church historians of any repute agree in
accepting it. We cannot claim even originality in teaching it in a Con-
gregational seminary. And we really feel guilty of a kind of anachronism
in writing an article to insist upon it. It is a point on which ancient,
mediæval, and modern historians alike—Catholic and Protestant, Lutheran
and Calvinist—have no controversy. And the simple reason for this
unanimity is, that the statements of the early fathers are so clear, and the
light shed upon these statements from the early customs of the church is so
conclusive, that no historian who cares for his reputation would dare to
deny it, and no historian who is worthy of the name would wish to.''
    In the face of such witnesses, need we say more?

NOTE C.—BAPTISM IN PATRISTIC AND PAPAL TIMES.

(1.) *The evidence of the Apostles' Creed—*
    The Apostles' Creed is one of the most precious heirlooms of the
Christian church ; and for the simplicity and directness of its affirma-
tions of the fundamental facts and conquering hopes of Christianity,
not surpassed by any literary fragment in existence. No prying and
unsatisfactory speculation mars it. The smoke of theological conflicts
does not hang over it. Minatory clauses do not convert it into an
unchristian imprecation. It is less like a high and battlemented castle
than the plain but ever attractive grounds and walls of the old home-
stead, where we spent our happy and careless youth, and formed all
our bright-winged fancies of the future. It is so thoroughly apostolic
in its ring, that it is the only portion of religious literature outside
the Bible that one would scarcely object to have printed with it.
    Grave doubts have been expressed as to the antiquity of this
document. Canon Swainson held that the Nicene Creed is older ;
others have brought the so-called Creed of the Apostles nearer
by several centuries to our times than it used to be put. But Dr.
Caspari, Professor of Theology in the Norwegian University,
establishes upon data of unquestionable accuracy and weight the
following important positions : —
    (1.) That the *Apostles' Creed* must have been that of the
church at Rome.
    (2.) That it cannot be of *later* date than the year 140.
    (3.) That there is nothing to prevent us from thinking that in

some of its parts it had been in use in Rome long before that—even at the time when Paul met the first Christians in the house of Aquila and Priscilla.

Of course, like other products of that sort, it has *grown*. The earliest form in which it is found exactly as it stands now is the eighth century. At the end of the fourth or beginning of the fifth century it, is much shorter than it is now—several clauses being absent.* Dr. Salmon† gives the fourth century form thus, the dash indicating an omission as compared with the eighth century or present form.

" I believe in God the Father Almighty——: And in Jesus Christ His only Son our Lord : who was born of the Holy Ghost and the Virgin Mary : under Pontius Pilate was crucified——: And the third day rose again from the dead : ascended into Heaven : sitteth at the right hand of——the Father—— : whence he cometh to judge the quick and the dead :

And in the Holy Ghost : the Holy——Church—— : the forgiveness of sins : the resurrection of the flesh—— :

The steps by which Caspari passes from Rufinus and Ambrose up to the Apostles are too long to be taken here. One point is, that the church at Rome had such strong regard for the Apostles' Creed that the decree of the Council of Nice could not supplant it. TERTULLIAN,‡ at the end of the second century, in his tract on the Soldier's Crown, says, that the Baptismal Confession was something more than of faith in the three Persons of the Trinity ; and that the addition was " sanctioned by *inveterata observatio ;* and from his writings it appears that the " something more " " included belief in our Lord's birth, crucifixion, resurrection, ascension, present sitting at the right hand of God and future coming, in the holy church and, in the resurrection of the flesh." So we are sure that baptized believers at the end of the second century confessed a faith similar to that, the express words of which we have as used at the beginning of the fifth.

But the creed itself warrants the inference of an earlier date.

---

* Rufuus wrote an Exposition of the Creed, which belongs to the first ten years of the fifth century. St. Ambrose, at a date a little earlier, maintained the apostolic origin of this Roman form of the creed.

† Contemporary Review, August, 1878.

‡ Born about 160, and died 245. Cf. De Bapt. 6, and Adv. Marc. v. 4.

The church is not *Catholic* in it. No emphasis is laid on the *oneness* of God, or the oneness of our Lord Jesus Christ. God is not described as maker of heaven and earth. The life everlasting is omitted. Had these been in at the first, it is fair to say they never would have been dropped out ; for those very points were in hot controversy at Rome after 140 A.D.

Hence Christian Baptism in the early days required the profession of Christian doctrine. It was not a mechanical act performed upon an unwilling and unwitting babe, but the expression of the soul's intelligent homage to Christ, and was preceded by an acceptance of the cardinal facts and truths of Christianity. Justin Martyr, whose account of the ceremonies of baptism is the earliest we have, witnesses that the candidates confessed their belief that the doctrines taught by the Christians were true, and made a promise to regulate their lives by the precepts of the gospel.

The place held by baptism in the beginning of Papistic times was this :—the sign of an intelligent acceptance of the truths of the gospel of Christ, and of a purpose to live to and for Him.

This is the witness of the earliest baptismal creed, the most venerable document the church has outside of the records which ought to govern her faith and practice in all things.

(2.) Novatian, a presbyter of distinction, took part in a vehement controversy in the church about the middle of the *third* century. His main contention was for the purity of the church, and one of his methods was antagonism to infant baptism. Numbers accepted his leadership, and *Novatians*, or Cathari, spread far and wide, planting Churches as far west as Paris, and, according to the historian Kurtz, establishing their communities almost throughout the whole of the Roman Empire.

(3.) Referring to the Donatists, Merivale in his *Lectures*, writes, " They represented the broad principle of the Montanists and the Novatians, that the true Church of Christ is the assembly of really pious persons only, and admits of no merely nominal membership." And as showing the continuity of this agitation and its connection with Baptist ideas, Hast observes (*Geschichte der Taufgesinnten*), " The doctrine of spiritual regeneration, the soul of Christianity, has perhaps never been taught with deeper feeling, and adhered to with greater zeal, than by the despised Anabaptists. Their aim was the highest possible,—a church of saints. Nowhere in church history is found such a subjugation of all other motives to the religious, such an approach to the order and life of the church of the apostles." And Jorg (*History of Protestantism*) testifies " that all the Anabaptists wanted was an entirely new church, a church of believers."

D.—BAPTIST CONTINUITY.

Barclay, in his comprehensive account of the *Inner Life of the Religious Societies of the Commonwealth*, declares (p. 12) " We have strong reasons for believing that on the Continent of Europe, small hidden Societies, who have held many of the opinions of the Anabaptists, have existed from the time of the Apostles. In the sense of the direct transmission of divine truth, and the true nature of spiritual religion, it seems probable that these churches have a lineage or succession more ancient than that of the Roman Church."

Another interesting witness may be cited. In the " *Origin and History of the Dutch Baptists,*" by Dr. S. Ypeij and Dermout (published in Breda, 1879), is the following:—" We have seen that the Baptists—those who in former times were named Anabaptists, and in latter days, Mennonites— were originally Waldensians, the men who in the history of the Church, in times so far back, have obtained a well-deserved renown. In consequence, the Baptists may be regarded as being from of old the only religious de- nomination that have continued from the time of the Apostles, as a Christian Society who have kept the faith pure through all the ages hitherto. The con- stitution, never perverted internally or externally, of the Society of the Baptists serves them as a proof of that truth, contested by the Romish Church, that the Reformation of Religion, such as was brought about, was necessary, was indispensable, and serves too as the refutation, at the same time, of the Roman Catholic delusive fancy, that their own is the oldest Church Society."

But it must not be forgotten that the *Dutch* Baptists were not Immer- sionists. They rejected infant baptism, but the mode of baptism adopted by them was *affusion* or *pouring*, and not immersion. MENNO SIMON, leader of the Dutch Baptists, taught that there is " not more than one baptism, viz., the baptism on belief;" but he speaks of that baptism as administered with " a handful of water." Hubmeyer, who established the Anabaptist Churches of Moravia, was also an affusionist, and, like Menno and Luther, came out from the Church of Rome retaining some of the Romish practices. The Anabaptists of the sixteenth century were in the main affusionists, though some of them taught the view of the *act* of baptism which became

N

established in England by John Smyth and his followers; so that when any one tries to establish Baptist continuity, it is very necessary that he should define with rigorous accuracy what is meant by the word "Baptist." And if he does that, it is not unlikely Baptist continuity will thin off into a most unsubstantial vapour. And what of that? If antiquity and continuity were "notes" of truth, Satan would have the advantage of all the denominations.

NOTE E.—EARLY ENGLISH BAPTIST CHURCHES.

Rev. J. J. Goadby, in his "Byepaths in Baptist History," recites and examines with skill and care the evidence in connection with the ancient Baptist Churches in England. He states that there is some probability that the chapel at *Hillcliffe* was built by Baptist Lollards. "One of the dates on the tombstones is 1357, the time when Wycliffe was still a Fellow at Merton College, Oxford," p. 22.

Eyethorne "owes its origin to some Dutch Baptists who settled in this country in the time of Henry VIII." This is a typical fact of that time. English Baptists are largely indebted to the Dutch.

NOTE F.—THE CROWLE CHURCH BOOK.

The Church Book, from which the statement is taken about John Smyth's Baptism, belonged to the Church at Epworth and Crowle, in Lincolnshire. The Rev. Jabez Stutterd, Minister at Epworth and Crowle, heard his deacons speak of the existence of this work; and being interested, found that it was in the possession of the Rev. Smith Watson, a minister at Butterwick, hard by. He obtained a sight of it, and discovered that it consisted of a few moth-eaten leaves, which had been given to Mr. Smith Watson by an old Baptist family of the district, who met with it in an old oak chest many years before.

Mr. Stutterd thought the pages might be of value, and the opinion of an expert, a skilled antiquarian, of the district was sought, and he reported as follows:—

"Nov. 9th, 1866.

"As keeper of the Manor-Charts of North-Lincolnshire, I have examined the Old Baptist Records, and believe them to refer to the last days of Queen Elizabeth and James the First. And recommend the friends connected with the Baptist Cause, to quickly copy them, or they will surely vanish away.

"F. CHAPMAN, Antiquarian."

The book was now guarded with jealous care, but at the request of the deacons, and with their aid, Mr. Stutterd made a number of extracts, and after some time forwarded them to me.

I was surprised at their contents, and specially at the statement concerning John Smyth's baptism, and asked to see the original; meanwhile Smith Watson had deceased, and the book could not be found. Search has been made again and again, but at present in vain.

The following document bears date December 16th, 1879:—

"We, the undersigned, Deacons of the Baptist Churches at Butterwick, Epworth, Crowle, having seen and handled the Old Records of seven or eight leaves, long before the Rev. J. Stutterd came into the County. And at our request and desire, and with our assistance, he copied the same moth-eaten records. We, as a Church, tendered him our sincere thanks, and requested him to send them to the Editor of the General Baptist Magazine for insertion.

"When copied, they were taken back to Butterwick, and consigned to the care of the late Rev. Watson Smith, and now we cannot, at present, place our hands on the document, or it would have been sent for Mr. Clifford's inspection.

"ANDERSON HIND.
"PETER GLOSSOP.
"JOHN CHAPMAN.
"BENJM. BATTY.
"GEORGE SINCLAIR.
"THOMAS SMITH.
"WILLIAM CHAMBERLAIN."

II. Now, what is the witness of the book itself?

(1) It contains a Church Covenant; date, January 4, 1599:—

"We, this Church of Christ meeting at Epworth, Crowle, and West Butterwick, in ye county of Lincoln, whose names are underwritten,* give up ourselves to the Lord, and one to another, according to ye will of God. We do promise and covenant, in ye presence of Christ, to walk together in the laws and ordinances of baptized believers according to ye rules of ye gospel, through Jesus Christ.— So helping us.

"JAMES RAYNER——JOHN MORTON, ⎫
"HENRY HELWISE——WM. BREWSTER, ⎬ Elders of ye Church."
"WILLIAM BRADFORD,   ⎭

* Thirty-two signatures or marks are given.

(2) It says, William Bradford "was baptized in ye old River Don below Epworth town, at midnight," Nov. 20, 1598.

(3) It speaks of persecutions and of efforts to get away to "Holland, where we hear there is freedom of religion for all men."

(4) It affirms that John Smyth, vicar of Gainsborough, enquired about baptism in Feb. 1604; was convinced of its truth, May 7; and baptized, March 24, 1606.

(5) It says, John Smyth baptized John Norcott, March 24, 1609.

(6) It records that at a meeting of the Church held on the 4th of April, 1609, "John Smith, John Morton, Henry Helwise, Richard Carver, Edward Winslow, William Bradford, James Rayner, William Brewster, Eli Kelsey, John Wood, all met to consult on removing ye church to Holland," and that, excepting James Rayner, Wm. Brewster, Eli Kelsey, and John Wood, they started on that night down the river Trent from Butterwick to Hull, and from thence to Holland; John Norton, who had not been baptized a fortnight, accompanying them.

(7) News arrives of the death of John Smith and John Norcott, through one, Thomas Petch, who returned from Holland to Crowle.

III. It is necessary very special caution should be taken in speaking of events belonging to the time comprised within this Church Book, and pre-eminently of such events as it was the business or pleasure of a Church scribe to record. We know but little of the details of the movements of persecuted Separatists in those days. Secrecy was a duty. Means of communication were scant to a degree we can scarcely imagine.

Moreover, the subject of "Baptism" was only just struggling into a defined position in the English life of the time. At first the Separatist members were not all averse to dwelling together in Church communion, though they held opposed views on the mode and subjects of baptism. That is clear even as far on as 1633, when John Spilsbury's Church was formed, or why cite as a reason for the formation of the Church—the fact that they were too numerous to meet together safely, and therefore might separate?

Remembering these points, is the Church Book account of John Smyth's baptism (1) consistent with what we know of his character? It is exactly what we should expect. There is the same caution, the same slowness, and then the same decision and courage we have seen in other portions of his career.

(2) Is it consistent with what he himself says in any writings of his? Does he anywhere say that he actually baptized himself? He says, in a book

published in 1609, three years after his baptism, *The character of the Beast, or the false constitution of the Church*, "The Anabaptists, as you call them, do not set up a new covenant and gospel, though they set up a new or apostolic baptism, which Antichrist had overthrown; and whereas, you say, they have no warrant to baptize themselves, I say, as much as you have [he was writing to a Brownist or Congregationalist] to set up a new Church, yea, fully as much. For if a new Church may be erected, which is the most noble order of the New Testament, much more may baptism," etc.

Here he is simply vindicating the right of Christians to set up a new Church on Baptist lines, if they think fit. That passage is no witness against the statement of the Crowle Church Book.

That this is the gist of the controversy appears from Robinson's words ("Of Religious Communion," works iii. 168), in 1614, "As I have heard from themselves. . . . . Mr. Smyth, Mr. Helwise, and rest, having utterly dissolved and disclaimed their former Church state and ministry, came together *to erect a new Church by baptism.*"

So if we look at other passages in the light of the fierce controversy of those times, we shall find that there is nothing in Smyth's statements which may not be explained by reference to his claim to the power of Christians to constitute a separate Church on the ground of baptism.

(3) But is not the Crowle book in violent collision with other testimonies? So it seems. The testimonies cited by Dr. Dexter (who writes as if he were at Amsterdam in 1608-14, and saw everything) to prove that John Smyth baptized himself, and that the Crowle record is a "feeble forgery," will carry conviction to some minds. But let us not forget, first, the prodigious facility of the Christians of those days in attack; secondly, the unutterable ignominy attaching to an Anabaptist, and the temptation to a controversialist to disparage an antagonist by charging him with acts thought opprobrious.

We have not space to report in detail our examination of Dr. Dexter's criticism, but we believe it will be found that the statement of the Crowle book not only fits exactly into Smyth's character, and is in accord with what he says about himself, but also may be reconciled with the allegations of others, concerning his baptism, when those allegations are interpreted by the light of the great question of the time, viz., the right to form new Christian Churches, and on what grounds.

Whether Smyth baptized himself, or was baptized in the river Don by another, is a matter of no importance whatever—except as a question of truth or error.

NOTE G.—JAMES ARMINIUS.

This accomplished scholar and gifted theologian was born in 1560, the year of Philip Melancthon's death, at the ancient town of Oudewater, in South Holland, midway between Rotterdam and Utrecht. He studied at Leyden with extraordinary ardour and success : gave his days and nights to theology, Hebrew, and mathematics, and took first rank amongst his fellow-citizens. In 1582, so conspicuous were his merits, the Merchants' Guild of Amsterdam sent him at their own cost to study at Geneva. There he heard Beza; from thence he went and studied and lectured at Basle, and whilst there visited Italy, and saw Popery in its native conditions and corruptions. In 1587 he began his ministry in the Reformed Church at Amsterdam, and gave full proof of his incorruptible sincerity, loyalty to truth and conviction, piercing intellect, warm heart, and high character. In 1603 he was appointed to the Professorship of Divinity in the University of Leyden, and he died October 9, 1609.

He was a true Reformer. Finding the Church in bondage to a cruel and false scholastic philosophy, and God's Word made void by the vain reasonings of men, he boldly set himself to break the chains and let the captive go free. He asserted the doctrine of General Redemption; and taught the actual, the real, and unreserved universality of the provision of salvation,—as to its source in the Father's love for all, as to its means in the Son's sacrifice for all, and as to its application in the Spirit's convincing work for all. He said :—" *There are two stumbling-blocks against which I am solicitously on my guard—not to make God the author of sin, and not to do away with the inherent freedom of the human will : which two things, if any one knows how to avoid, there is no action he shall imagine which I will not most cheerfully allow to be ascribed to the Providence of God, if due regard be only had to the Divine excellence.*" Those are golden words; and their defence was maintained at the risk of many years of ignominy and painful suffering, and in the face of bitter antagonism and personal loss. Arminius was of royal make, and he was willing to lay down his life for the truth. But he was more eager to *use* his life in embodying the truth. It is an egregious mistake which reduces him to a vigorous theological disputant. Grotius, who knew him well, says of him—

> " Subtle in intellect, and great in speech,
>   But careful most his life to regulate;
>   Arminius, dead, thus speaks, thus all would teach
>   (Of life approved, and matchless in debate)
>   I, as in life, in death this counsel give,
>   Be less disposed to argue than to live."

NOTE H.—GENERAL BAPTISTS AND LIBERTY OF CONSCIENCE.

In a Confession put forth in 1611, this luminous article occurs, "The magistrate is not to meddle with religion or matters of conscience, nor compel men to this or that form of religion; because Christ is the King and Lawgiver of the Church and Conscience."

Professor Masson, in his "Life of Milton," says, this is "the first expression of the absolute principle of liberty of conscience in the public articles of any body of Christians." Thomas Helwisse, who had the chief hand in drawing up this document, was Smyth's successor, and he drew around him some unforgettable men. Leonard Busher, who published the first English tract on Liberty of Conscience, in 1614, was one of his flock; and John Morton, who sent out a tractate entitled, "Objections Answered by Way of Dialogue, wherein is proved by the Law of God, by the Law of our Land, and by His Majesty's Many Testimonies, that no Man ought to be Persecuted for his Religion, so he Testifie his Allegiance by the Oath Appointed by Law," was his assistant. Thus, as Professor Masson says, "from a dingy meeting-house, somewhere in Old London, there flashed out first in England the absolute doctrine of Religious Liberty."

Dr. Dexter, in his *Congregationalism as seen in its Literature*, p. 102-3, cites the following words from Robert Browne: the magistrates "have no ecclesiastical authoritie at all, but onelie as anie other Christians, if so be they be Christians."

On this Dr. Dexter claims for him the proud pre-eminence of having been the first writer clearly to state and defend in the English tongue the true doctrine of the relation of the magistrate to the Church. Now Robert Browne wrote the above a generation before Busher's book appeared.

Professor Masson, describing the state of the Toleration Controversy in 1644, says (*Life of Milton, vol.* iii.):—

"The history of the modern idea of toleration could be written completely only after a larger amount of minute and special research than I am able here to bestow on the subject. Who shall say in the heads of what stray and solitary men, scattered through Europe in the sixteenth century, *nantes rari in gurgite vasto*, some form of the idea, as a purely speculative conception, may have been lodged? Hallam finds it in the 'Utopia" of Sir Thomas More (1480-1535), and in the harangues of the Chancellor of l'Hospital of France (1505-1573); and there may have been others. But the history of the idea, as a practical or political notion, lies within a more precise range. Out of what within Europe in the sixteenth and seventeenth centuries was the practical form of the idea bred? Out of pain, out of suffering, out of persecution; not pain inflicted constantly on one and the same section of men, or on any two opposed sections alternately; but pain revolving, pain circulated, pain distributed, till the whole round of the compass of sects had felt it in turn, and the only principle of its prevention gradually dawned on the common consciousness! In every persecuted cause, honestly conducted, there was a throe towards the birth of this great principle. Every persecuted cause claimed at least a toleration for itself from the established power; and so, by a kind of accumulation, the cause that had been last persecuted had more of a tendency to toleration in it, and became practically more tolerant, than the others. This, I think, might be proved. The Church of England was more tolerant than the Church of Rome, and Scottish Presbyterianism or Scottish Puritanism was more tolerant (though the reverse is usually asserted) than the Church of England prior to 1640. Not to the Church of England, however, nor to Scottish Presbyterianism, nor to English Puritanism at large, does the honour of the first perception of the full principle of liberty of conscience, and its first assertion in English speech, belong. That honour has to be assigned, I believe, to the Independents generally, and to the Baptists in particular.''

The principle of religious liberty is almost logically bound up with the theory of the independency of particular churches. Every particular church being a voluntary concourse of like-minded atoms, able to declare themselves converts or true Christians, it follows that the world, or civil society, whether called heathen or professedly Christian, is only the otherwise regulated medium or material in which these voluntary concourses or whirls take place. It follows that there must be large expanses or interspaces of the general material always unabsorbed into the voluntary concourses, and that for the secular power, which governs the general medium, to try to stimulate the concourses, or to bring all into them, or to control any part of the procedure of each or any of them, would be a mingling of elements that are incompatible, of necessary worldly order, with the spiritual kingdom of Christ. And so it was maintained against the Roman Catholics, and against the confessions of all the various established Protestant churches, that there could be and ought to be no Imperial or National Church. This being the principle of some of the early Protestant movements that went beyond Luther, Zuinglius, or Calvin, and perplexed these Reformers, little wonder that flashes of the fullest doctrine of liberty of conscience should be found among the records of those movements, whether on the Continent or in England. Little wonder, either, that the principle of toleration should be discernible in the writings of Robert Brown, the father of the crude English Independency of Elizabeth's reign.

To this passage Professor Masson appends the following note :—

See notices of such flashes among the English Baptists of the reign of Henry VIII., and among the Continental Anabaptists, in Mr. Edward Bean Underhill's "Historical Introduction" to the reprint of Old Tracts on *Liberty of Conscience* by the "Hanserd Knollys Society" (1846). Mr. Underhill writes as a zealous Baptist, but with judgment and research.

But Professor Masson also says :—" Passages which we have already had occasion to quote on the writings of Barrowe, Greenwood, and even of the liberal Robinson, the father of Congregationalism proper, prove beyond all dispute, that the chiefs of the Separatists and Semi-Separatists, who followed Brown in the latter part of Elizabeth's reign, and in the reign of James, had not worked out Toleration into a perfect or definite tenet. They did want something that they called Toleration; but it was a limited and ill-defined Toleration.

There is no doubt then that the General Baptists may, in the face of the present evidence, keep their forward rank as the first promulgators of the absolute doctrine of religious liberty.

NOTE I.—BAPTIST DECADENCE IN THE EIGHTEENTH CENTURY.

Ivimey says :—" There is no reason to doubt that our churches were far more prosperous and numerous at the Revolution in 1688 than at this period (1753) sixty years after, so that prosperity had, indeed, slain more than the sword." (*Hist.* iii. 279.)

But whilst Baptists declined in numbers, spirituality, and energy, in common with all other Christians during this century, *General* Baptists suffered most. Some of their leaders were specially disputatious, and persisted in controversy, whilst Kiffin, Knollys, and others, were "bewailing the state of their Churches," and fearing that "much of the former life and vigour which attended us is gone," that "Congregations had languished," and that they had neglected "giving that fit and proper encouragement for raising up of an able and honorable ministry for the time to come."

In addition to this, General Baptists, from three special causes, suffered most extremely.

(1) Their *centre* was rural and not metropolitan. This is a mistake they have never repaired, and from which they have suffered and suffer still. To work from *Fenstanton* might be inevitable in the days of Grantham; but it was blind and foolish in times of greater freedom.

(2) They received no accessions at the time of the "Ejection" from the more learned ministry of the established church, like their brethren who "denied Arminianism"; and in any time of theological crisis, a denomination led by men of well-disciplined minds will always suffer less than one that is under the guidance of men who lack effective scholastic training.

(3) Again, the "Generals" were slow to appreciate the worth of a trained ministry. The "Particulars" had a system for training men for the ministry as early as 1710. The General Baptist College only struggled into existence as the century closed.

If there be meaning in history, and if it is any advantage to live *after* the fathers, General Baptists ought to know what to do to repair their errors and redeem the time.

NOTE J.—WHAT GENERAL BAPTISTS BELIEVE.

The Denominational *Year Book* recites at length the Six Articles of faith and practice agreed upon by the fathers and founders, and states the Constitution and Laws of the Associated Churches. Those Articles do not contain *all* that is believed and taught; but, along with laws passed since, they signalize the special and distinctive features of our creed and polity of the General Baptists, viz. :—

I. THE DEITY OF THE LORD JESUS.

II. THE THREE GRAND UNIVERSALITIES OF THE GOSPEL REVELATION.

III. THE BAPTISM OF BELIEVERS BY IMMERSION.

IV. THE GOVERNMENT OF EACH CHURCH BY ITS OWN MEMBERS.

V. THE ASSOCIATION OF THE CHURCHES FOR THE PROMOTION OF SPIRITUAL LIFE AND WORK.

VI. THE RESPONSIBILITY OF EACH CHURCH MEMBER FOR THE HOLINESS, VIGOUR, AND GENERAL EFFICIENCY, NOT ONLY OF THE PARTICULAR CHURCH IN WHICH HIS OR HER MEMBERSHIP IS RECORDED, BUT ALSO FOR THE WELFARE OF THE MISSIONARY, EDUCATIONAL, AND LITERARY INSTITUTIONS BELONGING TO THE ASSOCIATED CHURCHES.

As to the Person and Rank of Christ they are in complete accord with the Evangelical faith as ordinarily understood.

On Baptism they teach that believers of any age are the fit subjects, and the *only* fit subjects; and that immersion is the New Testament mode; and, in virtue of this belief, they take their place in the Baptist Union of Great Britain and Ireland.

That which gives the title of *"General"* is their interpretation of the "Atonement." They hold and teach (1) *The Universality of the love of God to men*. "For God so loved the *world* that He gave His only-begotten Son, that WHOSOEVER should believe in Him should not perish, but have everlasting life." (2) *The universality of the redeeming work of the Son*. "For He is the propitiation for our sins; and not for ours only, but also for the sins of the *whole world*." Christ's death, the creed says, is a provision of salvation "FOR ALL THE SINS OF ALL MEN." (3) *The universality of the convincing work of the Spirit*. "When He is come He will convince the *world* of sin, of righteousness, and of judgment to come."

The sublime end contemplated in this wonderful manifestation, which is at once *one* and yet *three-fold*, is RIGHTEOUSNESS; an ever-active, tender, and strong love of right, fully displayed in God; and to be finally wrought out by His grace in man, His child.

This they maintain to be "the mind" of God; and fundamental to any true representation of the character of God. In their judgment God's saving work for the world is not restricted by any Divine decree, by any foregoing election, or any withholding of the convincing work of the Holy Spirit. Men are "lost," and continue so, for no other reason than that they will not be saved.

Note K.—Theological Changes.

"Among Evangelical Nonconformists, the severe and rigid lines of Calvinism have been gradually relaxed. Mr. Spurgeon stands alone among the modern leaders of Evangelical Nonconformists, in his fidelity to the older Calvinistic creed. The change became evident about the times of Andrew Fuller among the Baptists, and of Edward Williams among the Congregationalists. Edward Williams was a former pastor of this Church, and wrote a book, famous in its day, intended to reconcile what he called the Divine equity with the Divine sovereignty. My immediate predecessor, John Angell James, was a characteristic representative of the transition period. He was intensely Evangelical—loyal from the very core of his heart to the spirit of the Revival; and in his later days he was greatly depressed by the dangers which threatened the central articles of the Evangelical creed—the articles which are held in common by Methodists and Calvinists. But he followed with close interest the controversies which led to the temporary schism in the Presbyterian Church of the United States, and his sympathies and convictions went with the men of the "new school." Many of the old Calvinistic phrases were on his lips to the last, but the genuine Calvinistic meaning had gone out of them. The decay of Calvinism among Evangelical Nonconformists has been largely due to the influence of Methodism. John Wesley rendered us immense service by the vigour with which he asserted the moral freedom of man as against the Calvinistic doctrine of the Divine decrees, and the universality of the Atonement as against the Calvinistic doctrine which limited the relations of the death of Christ to the elect."

The Evangelical Revival, by R. W. Dale.

MORTON AND BURT, PRINTERS, 103, STAR STREET, PADDINGTON, W.

1.

OLD BRISTOL:

A STORY OF PURITAN TIMES.

Price 3s.

2.

THEODOSIA EARNEST,

Price 4s. nett.

3.

MISSIONARY SKETCHES.

By S. F. SMITH, D.D.

Price 4s. nett.

* Both of the above are the American Editions.

4.

PRINCIPLES and PRACTICES of the BAPTISTS.

By REV. C. WILLIAMS.

Price 1s.

5.

HOW TO READ THE BIBLE.

By REV. J. T. BRISCOE.

Price 2s. 6d. & 2s.

6.

ADVICE TO A YOUNG CHRISTIAN.

By REV. J. STOCK, LL.D.

Price 6d.

7.

THE BAPTIST VISITOR;

A Monthly Magazine. Interesting—Anecdotal—Expository.

For General and Local use.

BAPTIST TRACT AND BOOK SOCIETY,

CASTLE STREET, HOLBORN, E.C.

Fifth English Edition, enlarged to 587 Pages (Price 6s.)

THE TEMPERANCE BIBLE COMMENTARY;

BY

DR. F. R. LEES & REV. DAWSON BURNS, M.A.

The work gives at one view the Original Texts, the renderings of the principal Ancient Versions, with the criticism and exposition of about seven hundred passages in the Old and New Testaments bearing on wine and strong drink, or illustrating the principles of the Temperance Reformation; also answers to all objections. In addition to the Notes, there are a General Preface, a Preliminary Dissertation, Preface to the Notes, Essay on the connection between the Old and New Testament, many Appendices, and copious Indexes. The present edition contains a reprint of Dr. Kerr's "Unfermented Wine a Fact."

REV. DR. ANGUS (*one of the New Testament Revisers*).—"I am sure we shall find it of great value."

REV. DR. ROBERTS.—"A glance has been sufficient to excite my admiration. It is evidently a scholarly production, and I anticipate much pleasure from its perusal, whether or not I am able to agree with its criticisms and conclusions."

[LONDON; S. W. PARTRIDGE & Co., 9, Paternoster Row, E.C.;
and
ALLIANCE OFFICES, 52, Parliament Street, S.W.

---

332 Pages, with a copious Index, cloth gilt. (Price 5s.)

CHRISTENDOM AND THE DRINK CURSE;

An Appeal to Christians,

BY THE

REV. DAWSON BURNS, M.A., F.S.S.

The Fireside.—"The standard work on the Temperance question. All that need be said, if not all that can be said, is here said, and said well."

The Freeman.—"At once the completest and most elegant volume we have on this theme."

General Baptist Magazine.—"As persuasive as it is cogent, and as genial as it is forcible."

ALLIANCE OFFICES, 52, Parliament Street, London.

** Church Members, Superintendents, and Sunday School Teachers, will have a special reduction in price, by applying to Rev. DAWSON BURNS, M.A., with reference to either of the above Works.

Now ready. Crown 8vo., 448 pages, with PORTRAIT, *cloth boards, bevelled, price 6s. 6d.*

LIFE OF JAMES MURSELL PHILLIPPO,

Missionary in Jamaica.

By E. B. UNDERHILL, LL.D., Hon. Sec., Baptist Missionary Society.

OPINIONS OF THE PRESS.

" Dr. Underhill has selected his abundant materials with skill, arranged them with fine literary fact, and added to the number of religiously helpful and stimulating books one of the most interesting and instructive volumes."—*General Baptist Magazine.*

" In this goodly volume Dr. Underhill has furnished one of the most compact and complete, and, at the same time, one of the most fascinating biographies it has ever been our privilege to read."—*Baptist Magazine.*

" Will prove alike instructive and attractive to those who are interested in Missionary enterprize."—*Eastern Daily Express.*

" We thank Dr. Underhill for this remarkably cheap, but remarkably rich, contribution to our missionary biography."—*Freeman.*

" To a Baptist the volume will be delightful reading."—*Record.*

" Dr. Underhill has given us in this work one of the best biographies of one of the best and most honoured of modern Missionaries."—*Nonconformist and Independent.*

"Dr. Underhill's book is one which the friends of missions, and Baptists especially, will be delighted to read."—*Christian World.*

A most Valuable and Important Work on Baptism.

THE ARCHÆOLOGY OF BAPTISM,

By the late Dr. WOLFRED N. COTE, Missionary in Rome.

Price 10s. 6d.

" We could wish that a copy of this volume were on the book-shelves of every Baptist minister in England.—*Baptist Magazine.*

" Of great and permanent value."—*Freeman.*

Second Edition, handsomely bound in cloth, with Eight Illustrations, price 3s. 6d., post-free.

A SAVIOUR FOR CHILDREN,

By REV. JAMES DUNCKLEY, Upton-upon Severn.

" We most heartily commend Mr. Dunckley's book, and wish it a very large sale."—C. H. SPURGEON, in *Sword and Trowel.*

" Mr. Dunckley has a rare aptitude for the work of teaching young children the fundamental truths of Christianity."—*Nonconformist.*

" A copy should be placed in the hands of every child in the kingdom."—OCTAVIUS WINSLOW, D.D., Incumbent of Emmanuel Church, Brighton.

Large crown 8vo., cloth, price 4s., post-free.

MEMORIALS OF BAPTIST MISSIONARIES IN JAMAICA,

Including Sketch of the Labours of the Moravians, Wesleyans, and early American Teachers in Jamaica, Bahamas, Hayti, and Trinidad, and an account of the Presbyterian and London Missionaries' Societies' Missions. By JOHN CLARKE, Corresponding Member of the Ethnological Society, and late Missionary in Western Africa.

LONDON: YATES & ALEXANDER, 21, Castle Street, Holborn, E.C.
E. MARLBOROUGH & Co., 51, Old Bailey; and all Booksellers.

BAPTIST PUBLICATION BOARD.

THE GENERAL BAPTIST MAGAZINE.
Edited by Rev. John Clifford, M.A., LL.B., B.Sc., &c.
Published Monthly, price 2d.
Contains news of the Churches at home and abroad, and interesting papers on the topics of the day.

THE BAPTIST HYMNAL.
A new and beautiful Selection of Hymns for use in Families and Congregations.
Published in three sizes (large type, small type, and medium), and in prices ranging from 8d. to 8s., according to size and binding.

THE NEW BAPTIST SUNDAY SCHOOL HYMN BOOK.
ENTITLED,
THE SCHOOL HYMNAL.
Contains 343 choice Hymns for the Young.
Published in December, 1880, it has already been introduced into many Sunday Schools, and everywhere gives satisfaction.
Prices—Paper covers, 3d.; limp cloth, 4d.; cloths boards, 6d.; roan gilt, 1s.; Persian morocco, 2s.; cloth, red edges, gilt lettered, 8d.

INFANT CLASS HYMNAL.
A Selection of 89 Hymns from the School Hymnal, suitable for use in Infant Classes, and Services for young Children.
Prices—Paper covers, One Penny; limp cloth, Twopence.

In Preparation.
A TUNE BOOK
For the School and Infant Class Hymnals.

GENERAL BAPTIST PRINCIPLES,
An Exposition;
By Rev. Thos. Goadby, B.A., President of Chilwell College.
Price 1d.; a liberal allowance on quantities.

The General Baptist Year Book or "Minutes" for 1881.
Will be ready August 1st, containing Statistics and "Reports" of the Churches, Institutions, &c., of the Denomination. Price 6d.

The Publications named above, may all be obtained through any Bookseller ; or from
E. Marlborough & Co., 51, Old Bailey, London.

BY JOHN CLIFFORD.

Third Thousand. Crown 8vo., 132 pp., Boards, Gilt—Price 1s. 6d.

IS LIFE WORTH LIVING?
An Eightfold Answer.

THE ECHO.

" Mr. Clifford argues ably, ... proves himself a close observer of the various schools of modern thought, and grapples in earnest with the question."

CHRISTIAN WORLD PULPIT.

" Without shrinking from looking honestly at the evils and sorrows of life, without unduly minimising them for the purposes of argument, the author shows, and we believe convincingly, that . . . . there is an amount of happiness enjoyed by men on earth, and a measure of hope permitted as regards the future, which DO make life worth living. Mr. Clifford always writes as a man of culture and not less as one possessed by full and joyous faith in God. We sincerely trust that this volume will have a large circulation, for it is peculiarly adapted to the times."

BAYSWATER CHRONICLE.

" All the sermons are marked with an unusual wealth of intellectual culture and range of communion with the best minds, and, above all, by the stamp of a personal and hard-won experience in the wide field over which his subject takes him. The reader feels the unspeakable assurance that the author is living among the conditions which qualify him for his task and enable him to offer to others the help and strength he has acquired for himself. It will be many years before the subject outgrows the capacious intellectual and psychological treatment it has received at the hands of Mr. Clifford."

THE REV. C. H. SPURGEON IN THE SWORD AND TROWEL.

" A fine book . . . his work is well done, and is of a high order of literary effort, but we like best its firm faith and bright encouragement to souls half-blinded by the smoke of life's fierce battle."

GREENOCK DAILY TELEGRAPH.

" Mr. Clifford unites a rare power of popular exposition to richly varied scholarship, breadth of view, and of sympathy to evangelical fidelity and fervour. The work deserves, as we have no doubt it will secure, a wide circulation."

NORTH BRITISH DAILY MAIL.

" Thoroughly orthodox, but no less scholarly in substance and sympathetic in tone, as well as popular in form, it is admirably adapted for distribution among the modern race of doubters."

George Mostyn: A Tale for Young Christians.

Price 2s.

LONDON : PASSMORE & ALABASTER.

" It deals skilfully with various forms of doubt and religious difficulty, and is calculated to be of great service to youth in their first consideration of religious life. Every Sunday School library should have a copy."—*Christian World.*

" Well got up, and would make a nice New Year's gift.— *Baptist Messenger.*

Christianity in Rome.

A Sermon preached at the opening of the New Chapel in Rome.

Price 2d.

Religious Life in the Rural Districts of England.

Paper read at the Baptist Union.

Price 2d.

The Future of Christianity.

Sermon before the Baptist Missionary Society.

Price 3d.

The Attitude of Men of Science to Christianity.

Price 3d.

Jesus Christ and Modern Social Life.

Price 3d.

TRACTS ON BAPTISM; LORD'S SUPPER; AND THE CHURCH: By John Clifford, M.A.

2½d. the dozen, or 1s. 6d. per hundred.

"Need I be Baptised."

1d. each, or at the rate of 6s. per hundred.

The Place of Baptism in the Life and Teaching of Jesus.

Baptism a Privilege; or, the Place of Baptism in the First Ten Years of Church History.

"One of the best tracts on the subject; the church will do well to circulate it by hundreds of thousands."—*Baptist Messenger*.

The True Use of the Lord's Supper.

A New Testament Church in its Relation to the Needs and Tendencies of the Age.

The Church of Christ: Its Work, Character, and Message.

The Work of Church Members.

An Address from the Chair of the London Baptist Association.

The Surest Way of Bringing the Young to Christ.

The Church's War with National Intemperance.

Ninth Thousand.

"Thou shalt not Hide Thyself."

Sermon in Metropolitan Tabernacle for National Temperance League.

Romanism Judged and Condemned by Christ Jesus.

NEW TEMPERANCE PUBLICATIONS.

THE VOICE OF THE PULPIT ON TEMPERANCE. By Canon FARRAR, Rev. J. CLIFFORD, and other Authors. Cloth, limp boards, gilt, 1s. 6d.

THE VOICE OF SCIENCE ON TEMPERANCE. By various Authors. Cloth, limp boards, gilt, 1s. 6d.

RELIGIOUS AND EDUCATIONAL ASPECTS OF TEMPERANCE. By various Authors. Cloth, limp boards, gilt, 1s. 6d.

THE HISTORY OF TOASTING; or, Drinking of Healths in England. By the Rev. R. VALPY FRENCH, D.C.L., F.S.A., etc. Cloth, limp boards, gilt, 1s. 0d.

NON-ALCOHOLIC HOME TREATMENT OF DISEASE. By Dr. JAMES J. RIDGE. Cloth, limp boards, gilt, 1s. 6d.

THE TEMPTER BEHIND. By JOHN SAUNDERS, Author of "Abel Drake's Wife," etc. A powerful Story, dedicated to Dr. B. W. Richardson. Illustrated. Cloth, 3s. 6d.

HAROLD HASTINGS; or, the Vicar's Son. By the Rev. JAMES YEAMES, Author of "Inglenook," etc. Illustrated. Cloth, gilt, 2s. 6d.

PLUCKED FROM THE BURNING. A True Story. By LAURA L. PRATT, Author of "Our Sister May," etc. Illustrated. Cloth, gilt, 1s. 6d.

MISS MARGARET'S STORIES. By a Clergyman's Wife, Author of "Katie's Counsel," &c. Illustrated. Cloth, gilt, 1s. 6d.

THE JUVENILE TEMPERANCE SERIES of Short Stories, in three Packets. No. 1 contains Twelve little Books of 16 pp. each. Nos. 2 and 3 contain Six Books of 32 pp. each. 6d. per packet. These are also issued as **JUVENILE TEMPERANCE STORIES,** in two neat Volumes. Cloth boards, gilt, at 1s. each.

THE STANDARD BOOK OF SONG is really becoming "The Standard Book" for Temperance Societies, Bands of Hope, etc. The Words are published at 2d., 3d., and 6d.; and the Music Edition (in either Notation), at 3s. 6d. and 5s.; also in nine separate parts at 4d. each.
   The *Musical Times* says:—"The music is generally well chosen and excellently arranged throughout."

THE NATIONAL TEMPERANCE LEAGUE'S ANNUAL FOR 1881. Paper covers, 1s.; cloth boards, 1s. 6d. It should be in the hands of every temperance worker; it has been characterised as *the teetotaler's vade mecum.*

THE TEMPERANCE RECORD. The Organ of the National Temperance League. Published every Thursday. Price One Penny; post free, 6s. 6d. per annum.

THE NATIONAL TEMPERANCE MIRROR. An Illustrated Monthly Magazine for the Home Circle. Price One Penny: 1s. 6d. per annum, post free.

THE MEDICAL TEMPERANCE JOURNAL. Published Quarterly, price 6d. (free by post 2s. per annum).

A COMPLETE CATALOGUE OF TEMPERANCE LITERATURE. Comprising nearly all the known publications on the Temperance Question in Great Britain, and the various requisites of Temperance Societies of all kinds. Post free on application.

NATIONAL TEMPERANCE PUBLICATION DEPOT.
337, STRAND, LONDON, W.C.

187

www.ingramcontent.com/pod-product-compliance
Lightning Source LLC
Chambersburg PA
CBHW031954060726
47497CB00016B/2082